IN THE
NATIONAL INTEREST

General Sir John Monash once exhorted a graduating class to 'equip yourself for life, not solely for your own benefit but for the benefit of the whole community'. At the university established in his name, we repeat this statement to our own graduating classes, to acknowledge how important it is that common or public good flows from education.

Universities spread and build on the knowledge they acquire through scholarship in many ways, well beyond the transmission of this learning through education. It is a necessary part of a university's role to debate its findings, not only with other researchers and scholars, but also with the broader community in which it resides.

Publishing for the benefit of society is an important part of a university's commitment to free intellectual inquiry. A university provides civil space for such inquiry by its scholars, as well as for investigations by public intellectuals and expert practitioners.

This series, In the National Interest, embodies Monash University's mission to extend knowledge and encourage informed debate about matters of great significance to Australia's future.

Professor Margaret Gardner AC
President and Vice-Chancellor,
Monash University

SATYAJIT DAS
FORTUNE'S FOOL: AUSTRALIA'S CHOICES

MONASH
UNIVERSITY
PUBLISHING

Fortune's Fool: Australia's Choices
© Copyright 2022 Satyajit Das
All rights reserved. Apart from any uses permitted by Australia's *Copyright Act
1968*, no part of this book may be reproduced by any process without prior
written permission from the copyright owners. Inquiries should be directed
to the publisher.

Monash University Publishing
Matheson Library Annexe
40 Exhibition Walk
Monash University
Clayton, Victoria 3800, Australia
https://publishing.monash.edu

Monash University Publishing brings to the world publications which
advance the best traditions of humane and enlightened thought.

ISBN: 9781922633071 (paperback)
ISBN: 9781922633095 (ebook)

Series: In the National Interest
Editor: Louise Adler
Project manager & copyeditor: Paul Smitz
Designer: Peter Long
Typesetter: Cannon Typesetting
Proofreader: Gillian Armitage

Printed in Australia by Ligare Book Printers

A catalogue record for this book is available from the National Library
of Australia.

FORTUNE'S FOOL: AUSTRALIA'S CHOICES

The year 2020 was when COVID-19, date-stamped the previous year, entered our lexicon. The 2020 Tokyo Olympics and the Euro 2020 football championship would take place in 2021. The 250th anniversary of Ludwig van Beethoven's birth was to be celebrated on the 251st or 252nd commemoration. In Australia, the original date for the completion of vaccinations mysteriously disappeared from the political calendar.

A coronavirus of animal (zoonotic) origin was behind the disruption. An entire society predicated on the free movement of people, goods and services was brought to an abrupt halt. The virus brought the most sophisticated civilisation in the history of the planet to its knees, causing human and financial damage unseen outside of war.

In Australia, material comfort, security and distance from many global problems had made the nation complacent. The true bases of prosperity—a dependence on mineral exports; a dominant trading partner, China; and deferral of needed major reforms with their attendant costs—were not interrogated. Global shifts were overlooked. Policymakers competed to pander to the citizenry's illusions. Leadership meant avoiding electorally difficult decisions. That time has now passed.

The pandemic has exposed fundamental and largely ignored problems in Australia's society and economy, as it has in other countries around the world, which have accumulated over decades. It has become obvious that Australia may not have used its wealth and time well. Australians now face some difficult choices.

THE FOREVER VIRUS: THE COVID-19 SHOCK

Armchair Epidemiology

COVID-19 is highly infectious. The virus is transmitted mainly via respiration as infected people breathe, talk, cough or sneeze. Its effects range from cold or flu-like symptoms to pneumonia and respiratory failure. Most people experience mild-to-moderate symptoms and recover. It kills between 0.5 and 2 per cent of the infected, five to ten times influenza's mortality. People with underlying health conditions are especially vulnerable. Some suffer from, as yet, poorly understood long-term effects.

The World Health Organization (WHO) declared the initial outbreak a Public Health Emergency of International Concern on 30 January 2020 and a pandemic on 11 March 2020. With the disease poorly understood and no known vaccine or treatment, public health authorities resorted to medieval strategies. They used quarantine, a derivative of the fourteenth-century Venetian term *quarantena*, referring to the forty days for which all ships were isolated during the Black Death. Other measures included isolation, physical distancing and shutting public venues. There were restrictions on domestic and international travel, ranging from border screening and quarantine on arrival to total prohibition. Masks, washing hands and disinfection managed potential exposure. Testing identified infected individuals. Contact tracing allowed the tracking of infections to slow the spread of COVID-19. The objective was to contain the virus.

The first confirmed Australian case was identified on 25 January 2020. The man had returned from Wuhan, China, the original epicentre of the outbreak. Australian borders were closed to all non-residents on 20 March. Returning residents were required to spend two weeks in supervised quarantine, and Australians required special permission to leave the country. Through 2020, individual states and territories began closing their borders periodically to manage localised outbreaks. Social distancing, hygiene rules, contact tracing and testing became commonplace.

Man the Money-Printing Press

The pandemic, which at the time of writing has stretched over two years, has had significant costs. The public health expenditure has been large, the economic costs of the shutdowns and travel restrictions even larger.

The global economy shrank in 2020 by an unprecedented 5 per cent. Many countries experienced recessions—technically, two successive quarters of negative gross domestic product (GDP) growth. Australia experienced its first recession for nearly thirty years. Facing the largest slowdown in activity since the Great Depression, governments increased spending to bolster demand. Central banks cut interest rates and ensured ample availability of funds.

Just as controlling COVID-19 required slowing its transmission, policymakers sought to interrupt pandemic-induced economic feedback loops. The first concerned households, as unemployment, loss of income and falls in wealth reduced consumption. The second affected businesses, particularly in the services sector, which faced often precipitous declines in revenue and cash flow. These two pathways interlocked. Businesses downsizing or closing affected household income, which in turn lowered spending, further reducing economic activity.

Income support and improved unemployment benefits were aimed at households. Mortgage and rent deferrals sought to avoid evictions and foreclosures. Industry assistance packages provided businesses with cash grants and loans, as well as deferrals of rents, debt repayments, utility expenses and taxes.

There were parallel financial feedback loops. As asset prices initially fell, investors who had borrowed faced margin calls because the value of their collateral decreased. The inability to realise investments limited access to cash. Selling holdings or hedging against further falls pressured values, spreading the stresses into other markets. The concern was that these self-reinforcing cycles might result in a market crash. These financial and economic feedback loops then intersected. Declining investment income from lower rates and reductions in dividends, as well as difficulties in selling investments, decreased household cash resources and constrained spending.

Another financial feedback loop involved the banks. If the crisis intensified, then households, businesses and investors who were unable to repay their borrowings might default. Forced sales of collateral would affect asset prices. Reduced savings could decrease the deposits needed to fund banks. Rising bad debts and higher funding costs would cut bank earnings and capital reserves. This might decrease the willingness to lend or increase borrowing costs, affecting the credit-dependent real economy and investment markets. So central banks forced financial institutions to conserve capital by suspending dividends, providing temporary relief from regulations, and setting up special funding arrangements to make sure that banks had enough money to continue normal operations.

Central banks also initiated or increased existing quantitative easing (QE) programs, purchasing government debt with newly created currency. This assisted governments to finance spending and kept long-term interest rates low. Some central banks extended their QE programs beyond government debt, buying mortgage-backed bonds, corporate debt and also, in the case of the Japanese and Swiss central banks, shares. This supported prices, facilitated trading and stabilised markets.

Australia's response to the pandemic followed the global playbook. On 3 March 2020, the Reserve Bank of Australia

(RBA) cut interest rates, ultimately to near zero. Australia's federal and state/territory governments announced support packages for individuals, households, businesses and banks. These measures avoided an economic collapse and the associated human hardship that could have otherwise ensued, but the hurriedly created support packages were imperfect. Aid was misdirected. There were abuses. Programs sometimes duplicated each other. The suspension of debt servicing and allowing insolvent companies to trade risked creating future bad bank loans. Delaying scheduled payments or new loans sometimes only deferred the inevitable. If individuals could not find employment or businesses suffered permanent loss of income, then these amounts could prove irrecoverable.

Economic stimulus, according to one comedian, was the Australian Government returning money taken in the first place from taxpayers. If you spent the stimulus in shops, then the money went to China. Buying technology products benefited India, Taiwan or China. Buying a car helped Japan, Korea or Germany. Middle Eastern oil producers would profit from petrol purchases. Directing support packages to maximise economic effects wasn't simple.

By late 2020, the declines in activity had been stemmed. Economic growth rebounded, prompting hope for a 'V'-shaped recovery. Share and property prices rose sharply, exceeding pre-pandemic levels. But despite the progress, global economic output in many countries was projected to only return to pre-COVID levels by the end of 2022, barring any unforeseen setbacks.

The improvements were the result of massive government and central bank intervention. Direct measures were 5–24 per cent of 2019 GDP in advanced economies and between 1 and 9 per cent of GDP in emerging countries. Budget deficits increased sharply around the globe, contributing to the largest peacetime single-year increase in government debt-to-GDP ratios. In parallel, central banks had injected around 10–18 per cent of GDP through QE. Interest rates were zero or negative.

In the 2009 recession, the United States provided stimulus of about US$30–40 billion a month, roughly half the estimated output loss of US$80 billion a month. The 2020 stimulus, about US$150 billion a month, was three to seven times the estimated output declines of about US$50 billion in 2020 and US$20 billion in 2021. Combined injections of funds from governments and central banks, around 30 per cent of US GDP, generated 6–8 per cent in growth. An unsustainable $4 to $5 in new debt was now needed to create $1 in new income. Australia's position was similar, albeit less extreme.

Everywhere, authorities poured water into the leaking bucket at a rate greater than the losses, making it appear fuller than it really was.

Vaccine Hopes

By the second half of 2020, the discovery of vaccines offered hope: there were traditional vaccines using weakened or inactivated parts of the virus; newer messenger RNA (mRNA) vaccines taught human cells how to make a protein that triggered an immune response inside our bodies. The rapid rollout of a vaccine promised to end the pandemic, allowing resumption of normal life. The strategy was herd immunity, the amorphous and debated idea of a population resistant to the spread of an infectious disease based on pre-existing immunity of a high proportion of individuals as a result of previous infection or vaccination.

Certain conditions needed to be met. The vaccine had to be highly effective, durable and safe. Adequate supplies were needed. Distribution and vaccination programs had to be efficient. High acceptance and take-up of the vaccines was necessary. And the strategy had be global— no-one was entirely safe unless everyone was vaccinated. Mutations, especially more virulent or vaccine-resistant varieties, were assumed away. Perhaps predictably, the satisfaction of all requirements proved difficult in practice.

The vaccines generally were efficacious, reducing symptoms, the need for hospitalisation, and mortality. They were less effective in preventing infection and, importantly, stopping transmission of the virus. The duration of protection was unclear. Supplies were hampered by limited manufacturing capacity and shortages of raw materials. The need for cold storage for some vaccines and transport issues impeded distribution. The vaccination programs were slow due to the scale of the task.

While the majority of the population accepted the need for vaccination, some resisted. There was fear that the approvals had been rushed. Long-term side-effects were unclear. Alongside logical caution, a variety of ideological, libertarian, faux religious and quack objections (mind control, sterilisation) influenced attitudes. Evidence of side-effects, some fatal to a tiny minority, reinforced vaccine hesitancy.

Vaccine nationalism emerged. Developed countries had bought supplies of multiple vaccines sufficient to vaccinate their entire populations several times over, and they hoarded supplies at the expense of emerging nations. By mid-2021, developed countries were well advanced in vaccinating their citizens, while poorer countries had barely commenced their vaccination programs. In an epidemiologically, economically and morally dubious decision, in August 2021, many developed countries began offering booster shots—the WHO termed it giving extra life jackets to people who already had one.

In mid-2021, the Delta variant, which appeared first in India, quickly became the dominant strain. It was more contagious, more easily transmitted and possibly more deadly than other strains—additionally, many vaccines seemed less effective against Delta. Countries seemingly successful in controlling the virus earlier saw unexpected resurgences in infections.

Herd immunity requires high vaccination or infection rates: over 80 per cent or even over 90 per cent for more contagious variants. Even in advanced countries, these levels proved elusive due to plateauing vaccination levels, a reluctance to mandate compulsory vaccinations, and waning immunity as the effects of the vaccine diminished over time. Keeping eight billion people vaccinated permanently was practically difficult. Preventing transmission through isolation and quarantine measures was also becoming increasingly difficult due to the virulence of new strains, and the economic costs and problems of enforcing draconian lockdowns.

The Forever Virus?

Australia, initially, had a 'good' pandemic. Case numbers were brought under control, deaths weren't numerous, and localised outbreaks were dealt with successfully. The most serious was in Victoria, though largely confined to Melbourne, and eventually lasted almost four months. Things abruptly changed around June 2021, when community transmission from a single individual infected with the more virulent Delta version resulted in almost half of Australia's population having to be locked down.

This new outbreak proved difficult to contain. Confident in its position, Australia's vaccination rollout had been slow because a homegrown vaccine was abandoned, and the preferred, locally manufactured Astra-Zeneca vaccine was undermined by rare side-effects. Vacillating health advice and poor messaging caused confusion and hesitancy, while belated and poor procurement attempts slowed the supply of the mRNA vaccines. Underlying all this was hubris, encouraged by Australia's early success in the pandemic.

Like neighbouring New Zealand, Australia benefited from geography—it was an island at the end of the world. The strictest border controls in the world and rapid lockdowns were crucial to the countries' respective approaches. Epidemiologists convinced policymakers that controlling the virus and economic recovery were inseparable. However, resurgent infections illustrated the difficulty of containing the virus, with the Delta variant forcing both countries to go back into lockdown and defer reopening plans.

Australia and New Zealand also discovered that prolonged isolation from the world had a price. The economic costs, already large, escalated further. Activity plummeted, delaying the previously anticipated strong recovery. Trade and foreign investment were affected— for example, with interruptions and border controls likely to persist, Amazon shifted production of its *Lord of the Rings* series, one of the most expensive ever made, to the United Kingdom from New Zealand. Creating a hermit kingdom might stop the spread of the virus, but it condemned inhabitants to lower incomes.

The exhausted language shifted from eradication to containment to coexistence. Some Australian leaders sought to pivot away from 'zero cases': the idea that it was possible to eliminate the virus. The new approach was to tolerate case levels which the health system could accommodate. Desperate leaders privately sympathised with Brazilian President Jair Bolsonaro: 'I'm sorry. What do you want me to do? Miracles?'

COVID-19 will not be the last pandemic. Other diseases will emerge. Deforestation brings humans into contact with wild animals which carry exotic viruses. Crowded cities and leisure travel spreads contagious pathogens. Oceans, mountain ranges and deserts no longer provide natural barriers to the spread of diseases. Industrial live-stock production and poor public health provide fertile ground for mutations and new ailments.

As far as COVID-19 goes, there remain several possible scenarios. The virus dies out of its own accord. New and better vaccines and treatments reduce its impact. It becomes endemic, like influenza. Mutations remain a wildcard. As the reversals caused by the Delta variant illustrate, the pandemic may not be over, and the risk of continuing whiplash between opening, closing and reopening remains. The world, at least for the moment, is captive to the forever virus.

MAPPING MINEFIELDS: POST-PANDEMIC DYNAMICS

Fault Lines

The pandemic has exposed deep existing fault lines around the world. Even if COVID-19 hadn't done this, something else would have. The early response to the pandemic showed a lack of preparedness. Given the lengthy history of virulent pathogens, like SARS, MERS, H1N1, Swine Flu, Zika and Ebola, the outbreak should not have been unexpected. In developed economies, the lack of spending on health reflected austerity and poor planning. In developing countries, it was the lack of funds due to poverty, inept management, corruption and (in some cases) sanctions.

Buffers against shocks were inadequate. Households had limited savings, having borrowed heavily for housing and to finance consumption. Lower-income groups were victims of low wage growth, lack of employment security and inequality. According to the US Federal Reserve, many Americans would struggle to raise US$400 in an emergency. Meanwhile, according to the Grattan Institute, about 10 per cent of Australian working households had less than $90 to use in an emergency, and half of working households had less than $7000. Businesses and governments had limited financial flexibility to deal with a major crisis.

Borrowings compounded the problems. In the aftermath of the 2008 global financial crisis (GFC), everybody acknowledged the need to reduce debt. It just didn't happen. Low policy rates, abundant liquidity and rising house prices meant debt actually increased. Global debt as a percentage of GDP rose from around 250 per cent in 2007 to 325 per cent in 2019. As the pandemic hit, businesses and households, with declining or no income and high levels of borrowing, struggled to meet financial commitments.

COVID-19 also exposed weaknesses in global supply chains and just-in-time practices (where materials are not stored in advance but only supplied when needed). Infected workers, shutdowns in affected countries and interruptions to transport links derailed production— vulnerabilities that had already been highlighted by the 2011 Thai floods and the Fukushima nuclear reactor meltdowns. A dependence on imported goods created shortages, even affecting the initial public health response.

Lowering costs meant minimising surplus capacity, even in health care. Assumptions about being able to rapidly increase capacity ignored the time and cost of acquiring equipment and staff under crisis conditions. Call centres, including for essential services, relocated to developing countries, closed or operated at reduced capacity due to lockdowns or ill and absent staff.

Border closures restricted immigration and movement of labour. In many countries, agriculture relied heavily on itinerant foreign seasonal workers, usually from developing countries, so crops had to be abandoned in the fields due to lack of staff. Shortages of skilled foreign workers impeded many industries. Businesses relying on the free movement of people, such as tourism, education of overseas students, and medical procedures for foreigners, were badly affected.

In developed economies, personal services, particularly entertainment, leisure and travel, constitute a high proportion of activity. Any services requiring close personal contact were especially exposed to lockdowns. Services have an often overlooked weakness: they are non-storable and must be consumed when available. If a hairdresser is closed for a month, then the lost revenue from missed haircuts cannot be made up in the future; in contrast, a manufacturer of goods simply fulfils an order later provided the buyers are willing to wait. Loss of services revenue is permanent, making it more damaging for businesses forced to suspend operations.

In Anglo-Saxon countries, 40 per cent or more of the workforce are casual or contractors. Many small businesses, such as hairdressers, personal trainers and Uber drivers, are self-employment vehicles—the business is the person's job. This workforce is vulnerable to any inability to work, lacking protections such as sick leave or holidays, and with limited capital or reserves or access to finance. During the pandemic, many struggled to meet the requirements for state support, either receiving no assistance or getting help only after lengthy delays.

Since the 1980s the state has privatised many essential services, including health, telecommunications, utilities and, sometimes, emergency services. The pandemic revealed that many private businesses, sometimes foreign owned, did not act in a way that was consistent with a nation's interests. Procuring and distributing ventilators, personal protective equipment and even basic medical consumables, for example, became problematic.

The pandemic also exposed the effects of inequality, within and between nations. In richer countries, poorly paid workers, often employed in essential sectors, were basically daily wage earners who lived payday to payday. They could not afford to isolate. Income disparities and unaffordable housing meant that they lived in distant suburbs in often substandard and crowded accommodation. They became vectors spreading the virus.

Developing countries lacked adequate public health resources to deal with even routine needs. Total healthcare spending in these nations, home to around half the global population, was less than half the 14 per cent average of GDP in developed economies. On a per-individual basis, they spent a mere 5 per cent that developed nations expended. High population density, slums, poorer general health and lack of sanitation made implementing pandemic-control measures impractical. Vaccine unavailability aggravated these failings, making controlling the virus globally nearly impossible. And so it continued to circulate, providing a breeding ground for mutations.

Australia was vulnerable to many of these factors. A key issue the pandemic exposed was a dependence on foreign workers. Border closures translated into a shortfall of more than 150 000 workers, which slowed any economic recovery. Farm workers, hospitality and mining staff were in short supply. There was a dearth of engineers, scientists and other professionals who were needed in priority sectors, such as infrastructure and advanced industries. Australia also found itself affected by the disturbance of global supply chains. The nation's glaring inequalities became obvious, retarding efforts to control COVID-19.

Damage Report

As reality set in, governments everywhere assessed the damage.

The pandemic has been expensive. The total cost to the United States of COVID-19 for 2020 alone was estimated at US$8 trillion, just under 40 per cent of GDP. That is four times that of the GFC–induced recession. Australia lost a more modest $200 billion to $300 billion, around 10–15 per cent of GDP initially. The 2021 resurgence resulted in large but as yet indeterminate additional costs. This ignores less easily quantifiable effects, such as damage to economic potential as well as social costs, including premature death, physical and mental health impairment, increased inequality and damage to student learning.

There has been wealth destruction from drawdowns in savings and falling values of investments. During the GFC, the United States alone lost around US$10 trillion. By December 2020, three million Australians had withdrawn $36 billion of their retirement savings. Savings depleted because of the COVID-19 crisis will affect future consumption levels. Low interest rates fuelling rises in share and house prices may restore wealth for some, but the adverse effects will be marked for disadvantaged socioeconomic groups, with their lower savings and less in the way of financial investments.

Given that the pandemic is not over and considering difficulties of measurement, the true cost of COVID-19 will simply not be known for a long time. But it is already clear that a major legacy of the pandemic will be an increase in already high global debt levels. Global debt-to-GDP surged in 2020 by 35 per cent—the largest annual increase on record, greater than the 10 per cent rise in 2008 and that of 15 per cent in 2009 after the GFC. In OECD countries alone, government debt levels increased from 109 per cent of GDP to more than 137 per cent. Total global debt continued to climb in 2021, reaching nearly US$300 trillion, around 350 per cent of global GDP.

Australia's total debt levels are around 300 per cent of GDP. Government debt is rising but still ostensibly low at about 40 per cent. However, this ignores rapidly increasing borrowings by state and local governments, as well as major contingent liabilities flowing from the support of government corporations and private–public partnerships supplying essential infrastructure and services. And it overlooks implicit government guarantees for Australia's too-big-to-fail banking system, which is heavily exposed to households carrying one of the world's highest debt burdens, primarily driven by inflated house prices.

Public-sector debt increases reflect higher healthcare spending, actions taken to alleviate the economic effects of the crisis, emergency loans and lost tax revenues. Households and businesses have substantially increased borrowings to cover falls in income. With around half of government-support packages structured as loans or payment deferrals, indebtedness has grown substantially. If the recovery is slower than expected, then the rise will be greater.

For households and businesses, the need to meet debt obligations will restrict future spending and investment. Low rates and central bank funding via QE enable governments to increase debt for the moment. However, with debt likely to reach 150 per cent of GDP in many countries, it will retard growth, reduce spending flexibility and crowd out other borrowers. Low future growth rates and high debt levels are incompatible and will ultimately weigh on prospects.

Business will be slow to recover. Inadequate reserves, lost invested capital, lack of new funds or unwillingness to reinvest mean that some will fail. Closures will destroy the proprietary knowledge embedded in ecosystems of customers, staff and processes. Those ventures that continue to operate may have to radically restructure operations or reduce their scope and scale.

Tourism and hospitality businesses, especially airlines, have crisis liabilities. They did not refund cancelled bookings but provided credits for future use to conserve cash. If and when they honour these obligations, they will incur costs in providing the service but without receiving any new revenue.

Negative effects in the labour market will persist. Employers will recalibrate the workforce for greater flexibility to protect against future shocks. This will increase casualisation and subcontracting, and decrease job security and incomes. The effects will fall mostly on the low-paid, women, minority groups and immigrants. In turn, without realistic prospects of getting work, many will leave the workforce, depriving the economy of expertise and experience—one of Australia's best wildlife guides had to advise his clients that he had been forcibly retired by government restrictions. A core of long-term unemployed with depreciating job skills may never be re-employed, increasing the demand for welfare and incurring large social costs.

Scarring from the crisis may also affect family formation and fertility, which may reduce population growth, exacerbating the pressures of Australia's ageing population. Attitudes towards spending and saving may also shift. After the Great Depression, fearing the onset of a new crisis, people became thriftier and more cautious.

An economy is a complex, highly coupled system. The act of removing a large number of businesses and the corresponding jobs for extended shutdowns has a detrimental effect which will only reverse slowly. One reason why national economies will have difficulty restarting is that the world economy was in poor shape even before COVID-19 actually hit.

Crises (Plural)

When the pandemic began dominating headlines, the world was already approaching environmental and resource limits that pose existential threats to society.

The effects of human activity on climate have been known since at least the 1950s. Central to this is the use of fossil fuels. Carbon dioxide (CO_2) emissions are currently at record levels, up 50 per cent since industrialisation and up 11 per cent since 2000. And the impacts of climate change are accelerating due to complex feedback loops and pulse events, where chains of large adverse effects are triggered. Irreversible tipping points may already have been reached.

Climate change is driving record high global temperatures, the primary consequences of which include more intense and frequent droughts, floods and wildfires, and rising sea levels. By 2050, 480 million people may be exposed to potentially lethal heatwaves. Sea level rises are also quickening due to melting ice sheets, which could displace 600 million people by mid-century.

The world faces rising resource scarcity. Global water demand has increased six-fold over the past century, and it is projected to rise 50 per cent by 2050 because of population growth and more water-intensive lifestyles. But the industrial pollution of water sources and the effects of climate change constrain supply. Around 1.7 billion people, nearly a quarter of the world's population, now experience extremely high levels of water stress—that number will double in the next few decades.

Food production must increase 60–100 per cent by 2050 to feed mankind. It is under pressure due to limited arable land, degraded soil quality, rising salinity, water shortages and peaking crop yields; 90 per cent of all fish species are either fully or overfished. About two billion people (26 per cent of the world's population) now experience some form of food scarcity. At the same time, one-third of all food produced, 1.5 billion tonnes annually (worth around US$1.2 trillion), is wasted.

The effects of ongoing climate change and resource scarcity on Australia will be significant. The continent is naturally hot and dry, and higher temperatures will make parts of Australia uninhabitable. There will be serious health consequences, as rising deaths from extreme Northern Hemisphere heat waves have illustrated. The increase in temperatures will affect industry and infrastructure, like electricity supply and transport links. As recent experience shows, longer and more testing wildfire seasons will affect land use. And with most of Australia's population based on the coast, even a small rise in sea levels will impact habitability; some parts of Australia and certain activities may become commercially uninsurable.

Agricultural production and livestock will be affected by more frequent and severe droughts and floods.

Unpredictable rainfall, damaged river systems and falling aquifer levels will reduce food sufficiency and export incomes. Water supply constraints will impact lifestyles and industrial activity, with rationing probable.

Climate change will also diminish the allure of tourist attractions. The Great Barrier Reef, the largest living structure on Earth, supports 64 000 jobs and contributes $6.4 billion to the Australian economy. Dredging for shipping access, algal damage from fertiliser run-off, invasive species, warmer seas, ocean acidification and altered weather patterns now threaten its survival.

The financial damage caused by climate change will be substantial. The forecast annual cost for Australia is between $100 billion and $200 billion, or 5–10 per cent of GDP. A coalition of central banks, including the RBA, has estimated that around a quarter or more of global GDP could be lost by 2100. Much of these losses will be from infrastructure damage, falling property values, lower agricultural and labour productivity, and failing biodiversity and human health.

In addition, Australia will need to cope with increasing numbers of climate refugees and instability arising from resource competition.

A New Playing Field

Several important trends, some of which were evident before COVID-19, will shape outcomes in the post-pandemic world. Future economic growth, already having slowed for decades, is likely to be low and volatile.

Expectations of continuously improving living standards may require adjustment. The impacts of opening economies to trade and investment and the advent of computers and the Internet are waning. An economy based on purchasing unnecessary things for unknown reasons with borrowed money is proving to be unsustainable. The effects of deregulation and financialisation, primarily borrowing and speculation, are reaching their limits.

The free movement of goods, services and capital was an important catalyst in economic growth, improving living standards and lifting large numbers of people out of poverty. But the unequal sharing of benefits has made it unpopular amongst those it has disadvantaged and politicians seeking the restoration of sovereignty. The pandemic has highlighted the need for greater national control over strategic industries and essential goods and services.

Events are fast-tracking the existing drift towards autarky; that is, closed economies. Governments are becoming more domestically focused, believing that this will capture a greater share of the available economic activity, deliver greater prosperity for citizens and improve the effectiveness of policies. Trade restrictions, capital controls, manipulation of the currency, discriminatory regulatory regimes and sanctions increasingly retard cross-border commerce and access to technologies and finance. As a result, globalisation will slow or, in some areas, reverse. Rather than trade and investment, the focus may become virtual or digital, around the growth of data and information sharing via digital platforms.

At what is hopefully the tail end of the pandemic, actual and expected inflation have risen sharply, although remaining low in historical terms; some of this reverses the sharp falls during the early phase of the pandemic. A large increase in commodity prices is one factor. Oil prices have tripled from lows of around US$20 per barrel because of a recovery in demand as well as a temporary abatement in disputes between producers which led to oversupply. Food prices are also higher, up around 40 per cent, due to climate change–driven weather conditions, disease, and plagues of locusts in East Africa and the Middle East.

Higher inflation also reflects pandemic-induced supply chain disruptions. Semi-conductor shortages have slowed vehicle production, leading to large increases in used-car prices. Transportation costs are higher: container shipping costs, for example, have increased dramatically due to lack of capacity and difficulties in sourcing crews from developing nations during the pandemic. Inflation expectations include wage pressures due to labour shortages in some sectors—travel restrictions as well as post-pandemic shifts in economic structure have contributed to this.

Policymakers claim that inflationary pressures are temporary, although some confess that there may be 'longer-lasting transitory factors'. They argue that demand for the materials and products needed to combat COVID-19 will ease and overly generous short-term government income support will be withdrawn. But the large infrastructure programs introduced to assist recovery will boost demand for years.

Furthermore, current inflation reflects primarily supply factors and input costs that may persist. Higher property prices will feed into housing costs and rents. Businesses will need to recover pandemic losses and repay borrowings incurred during the crisis. Additional post-COVID-19 occupational health and safety requirements, barriers to trade, and national control over strategic supplies and products may lead to a structural rise in costs. The effects of climate change and scarcity on prices may prove material, too. The potential confluence of low growth and inflation would be an unwelcome rerun of 1970s stagflation.

The pandemic will quicken changes in economic structure. There will be less emphasis on mobility and more activity will shift online. The labour market will change with the accent on remote work and demand for different skills. The adoption of technologies such as robotics, automation and artificial intelligence (AI) will eliminate perhaps a third to a half of all jobs. This will create more tiered societies: a small group of well-paid, in-demand workers; a large supporting precariat of piece workers in the casual and gig economy; and an unemployable underclass. Given the reliance of the global economy on consumption, the changes will affect economic activity. In parallel, control of these technologies, which are highly mobile and generally not location-specific, will be fiercely contested.

Developed countries will see slower population growth. An ageing citizenry will place new demands on health and aged care. Worker shortages in some countries and sectors will emerge. An increased focus on sustainability in response to environmental pressures is inevitable, although its form remains uncertain.

There will be a rebalancing of the roles of the market and state—big government is back. Budget deficits will continue. Public debt will rise. Continued government spending will require, at some stage, higher taxes or expanded financing by central banks. Greater state intervention will alter the structure of risk bearing. Bailouts may reduce competition and create industrial zombies as governments preserve firms and employment. Central bank support will encourage investors to assume that downside exposures are underwritten.

The established differences between political constituencies will also increase. Key areas of conflict will include the role of government and personal rights in a period of greater social control and surveillance technologies.

Internationally, there is the return of competition between familiar empires: the United States, China, Russia. Differences in political systems, histories and relative power make agreement on important matters difficult. Given that many of today's challenges are global in scope, such as the pandemic and climate change, coordinated action is becoming increasingly difficult.

Cognisant of the need to offer hope, and with an eye on their electoral futures, leaders and policymakers everywhere are promising, like President Biden, to build back better. In increasingly uncertain times, this will require the reformation of Australia's industrial structure, realignment of its geopolitical and trading relationships, the development of new policy ideas, and concentrated efforts to overcome political paralysis.

HOUSES AND HOLES: THE AUSTRALIAN ECONOMY

Model Engines

For most ordinary citizens, the economy is simply the engine that delivers jobs, housing, life's needs, social services and retirement. Economic growth ensures rising living standards and a better future. National prosperity depends on natural endowments; population, especially workers, their skills and productivity; and the availability of capital. It comes from consumption, investment and net exports, what we sell to foreigners less what we buy from them. Each nation's economic model seeks to manage these elements to their best advantage relative to competitors.

Australia's economic performance has been driven largely by its bountiful natural resources. After European settlement, the first chapter of this performance entailed riding on the sheep's back. Farming and livestock made Australia one of the richest countries on earth—it benefited from abundant land, low costs, and global demand for items like high-quality wool and meat. The second chapter, what journalist Paul Kelly dubbed the 'Australian settlement' (the nation-building that occurred from Federation), sought to reduce the dependence on primary production. The focus was on creating an industrial sector, behind a wall of tariffs and subsidies limiting foreign competition.

The third chapter entailed opening up Australia's economy to a rapidly globalising world. The key steps in this were phasing out industry assistance, deregulating the financial sector, market-determined exchange and interest rates, the privatisation of government assets, freeing up labour markets, and mandatory retirement savings. Throughout, agriculture and the mining industry have remained prominent.

Australia, today, is a houses and holes economy. During part of the economic cycle, activity is based on residential property and construction (the houses). At other times, national income and prosperity are driven by commodity exports (the holes). Supported by a growing services sector, this model has ensured high living standards—Australia's growth record up until the pandemic was exemplary.

Boom-ier Booms

Australia has experienced several mining booms, starting in the mid-nineteenth century. The original boom was driven by the California gold rush, which began in 1848, and inflows of international capital. In the twentieth century, there were booms in the 1970s (coal, iron ore, oil, bauxite) and the 1980s (energy, primarily steaming coal, oil, gas and aluminium smelting). The latest episode (iron ore, coal and gas) is ongoing. The last two booms have been driven by the economic rise of Japan, China and India.

The booms have created wealth and also shielded Australia from downturns. The 1970s boom helped offset the concurrent oil shocks, while the most recent instalment protected Australia from the dotcom crash and the GFC. In 2020, mineral exports reduced the economic impact of the COVID-19 pandemic.

Mineral booms follow a specific pattern. In the first phase, growing demand for a commodity increases prices and export incomes. The second phase entails investment to scale up production to meet forecasts. The final phase is production, when revenue from commodity sales commences. These booms affect living standards by boosting national income, creating jobs and increasing wages. Growth in mining also obviously benefits the construction industry and utilities (power, gas, water, logistics, transport). Rising investment income (rent, interest, dividends) increases disposable income, while higher tax revenues and royalties allow greater public spending or tax cuts, increasing growth and household income.

During the most recent boom, Australian resource-sector investment peaked at close to 9 per cent of GDP, about five times historical levels. It boosted overall employment by around 3 per cent and wages by around 5 per cent. Overall household disposable incomes were around 10 per cent higher.

Property Ladders

Housing in advanced economies is more than shelter. It is an investment asset, used to accumulate and store wealth. You purchase a house which rises in value, increasing your equity—the current value less the amount owed on the mortgage. You later upgrade, selling your existing house and buying a more expensive property with more debt. When the new property appreciates, you repeat the process. This activity extends to speculative transactions. People from all walks of life borrow money to purchase properties to profit from rental income and expected price increases.

Alongside retirement savings, the value of your home or investment property has become an important source of wealth. Borrowing against its value finances spending. The assets fund post-work life and provide a legacy for your progeny.

The importance of housing is reflected by Australia's high level of home ownership, which at 65 per cent is comparable to the United States and United Kingdom, but is 15–20 per cent higher than Germany, Switzerland and many Asian trading partners. Construction provides local, well-paid jobs. And governments can influence activity through a variety of levers: incentives, subsidies, the release and zoning of land, as well as interest rates and finance availability.

A substantial part of the economy is now founded on residents buying property from and selling it to each other or foreigners for ever-higher prices using borrowed money. It is a surreal pyramid of paper wealth creation.

Australian Miscellany

These primary engines are supplemented by other factors.

Australia has one of the highest population-growth rates in the developed world (around 1.5 per cent per annum), driven mainly by immigration that is focused on skilled labour to enhance the workforce. A proportion are those who arrive under the significant investor visa scheme, which is available to entrepreneurial and wealthy individuals able to commit at least $5 million. The program attracts 10000–12000 entrants in a typical year, many from politically unstable countries looking to safeguard their wealth. This growing population feeds economic activity.

A varied services industry has also emerged, employing nearly 80 per cent of the workforce. It focuses on health, aged care, education, hospitality, leisure activities and personal services—some concentrating on export markets. Australia's well-regarded healthcare system seeks to attract foreigners from nearby countries, especially for complex procedures. However, high costs and capacity issues mean that it lags medical-tourism destinations such as Singapore, Thailand and India. Instead, many Australians now travel overseas for treatment on the grounds of cost and speed.

Australia fares better in other areas. Tourism constitutes around 3 per cent of GDP (about $60 billion) and is an important contributor to regional economies. It is Australia's fourth-largest export industry, comprising around 8 per cent of Australia's export earnings. It employs around 700000 people and relies on natural assets, a safe and clean environment, and proximity to Asia. International education—foreign students studying in Australia—is now Australia's third-largest export after iron ore and coal, supporting at least 250000 jobs.

The oversized Australian financial sector employs around 800000 people and contributes around 8 per cent of GDP. Bank assets are around 130–140 per cent of GDP, a five-fold increase over the last fifty years, and double the US and global average. This reflects the credit-intensive nature of housing and the mining industry. Underpinned by a mandatory retirement savings scheme, Australian superannuation assets now total over $3.1 trillion, one of the largest such pools of money in the world.

Infrastructure spending is used to smooth out activity. This entails the renewal and expansion of energy, water, gas, transport, telecommunications and community amenities, in part to accommodate larger populations.

One notable absentee is manufacturing, which has declined from a high of almost 30 per cent of GDP in the 1950s to around 6 per cent today. The fall is exaggerated by an artificially elevated starting point reliant on previously high trade barriers. Australian manufacturing is bedevilled by a small domestic market, locational disadvantages and high costs. Automobile production effectively ceased in 2017, despite generous government life support. Australian textile, clothing and footwear manufacturing, substantial until the mid-1980s, has largely shifted to cheaper Asian countries. Australia now produces two-thirds of the amount of manufactured goods it consumes; in contrast, many developed nations produce surpluses.

Falling into Holes

The economic structure that has evolved is narrow and risky. The dependence on commodities exposes the economy to volatile price cycles. The virtuous sequence of higher prices, investment and production can reverse viciously. Overzealous demand projections, overinvestment, competition and political influences can quickly turn booms into busts.

Over the last fifteen years, iron ore prices have fluctuated between US$40 and US$220 per tonne. Over a similar period, thermal coal prices have oscillated between US$50 and US$170 per tonne. Oil prices have ranged between US$10 and US$140 per barrel. Natural gas prices have moved between US$1.60 and US$14 per metric million Btus (British thermal units).

This volatility doesn't just affect business earnings but also government revenues. In 2012, Western Australia and Queensland experienced sharply lower mining royalties. In early 2021, buoyant prices for iron and coal initially provided a large bonus, but as the end of the year approached, falling prices again reduced public incomes. The sensitivity of government revenue to the iron ore price is substantial: a US$10 per tonne rise in prices increases Western Australia's royalties by around $800 million per year.

Australia's mining wealth is narrowly based around large iron ore, coking and thermal coal, and, increasingly, liquid natural gas (LNG) projects, which exploit non-renewable, finite resources. Barring new discoveries, the economic reserves of iron ore, at current production rates, will last around fifty to seventy years; the comparable figures for coal and LNG are around 100 and sixty years, respectively. Production lives may shorten because as low-cost reserves are depleted (for example, the Pilbara iron ore and Bowen Basin coal reserves), Australia's competitiveness, plagued by high cost structures and a poor record of expense management, will decrease.

Australia's fossil-fuel energy exports will be affected by measures to reduce carbon emissions. Shifts to renewables, proposed taxes and levies, such as that suggested by the European Union (EU) on carbon-intensive imports, will affect demand and earnings. Resource assets may become stranded, with clear implications for investors and financiers. Anticipatory action taken by capital providers means that many miners, especially medium-sized and smaller firms, already face difficulty raising funds.

Australia has not saved the proceeds of booms to smooth out commodity price cycles or to invest for a post-mineral future. Options rejected include a sovereign wealth fund or legislation, such as Chile's fiscal responsibility law, which restricts governments from spending temporary mining revenue windfalls.

Mining projects are capital-intensive. Much of the equipment, technology and capital must be imported, affecting Australia's external finances. For most of recent history, the current account has been in deficit. Australia must attract overseas money to finance the gap.

Resources directly account for around 2–3 per cent of total jobs. Construction requires local labour with attendant economic benefits. However, skill considerations, shortages and often remote locations mean that imported workers are frequently used. High levels of mechanisation and automation mean less labour is required once projects are operational. Meanwhile, new technologies such as floating LNG plants, manufactured and assembled in more cost-effective locations and towed into place, may similarly affect job creation. The technology unlocks stranded gas, avoids land-access issues, reduces local infrastructure bottlenecks, decreases secondary costs like worker housing, and has lower decommissioning costs. However, it offers less economic benefits to the host country than conventional projects.

Australia's mining industry is over 80 per cent foreign-owned. A 2016 Treasury paper found that less than 10 per cent of mining projects underway at that time were solely Australian-owned. Major listed entities like BHP and Rio Tinto are 70–80 per cent foreign owned. This means earnings from projects flow overseas rather than remaining in Australia. Large write-offs, depreciation, capital allowances and avenues for cross-border planning means that the local tax revenue take is limited. The need to service foreign capital in the form of dividends and interest affects Australia's current account.

Other Vulnerabilities

A dominant resources sector can distort the economy, a process termed the 'Dutch disease', originally describing the decline of the Netherlands's manufacturing sector after the discovery of large natural gas fields. A booming mining sector monopolises capital and workers, and pushes up cost structures and the value of currency, reducing a nation's competitive position. For example, a high Australian dollar disadvantages agricultural exports, which are also affected by biblical cycles of drought, flood and pestilence. A strong currency and expensive products also discourages overseas travellers, and simultaneously encourages wanderlust-prone Australians to travel overseas.

Educational and tourism exports suffer from other problems. The highest-ranked antipodean university in global standings is the Australian National University, at number twenty-seven. In any case, the best, most affluent students favour the top North American and European schools due to perceived stronger programs and better networking opportunities. The expansion of the sector has seen an upsurge of institutions and programs of variable quality and legitimacy. This growth, in part, is linked to loopholes in migration rules and the sector's utility as a source of low-cost casual workers. The cross-subsidisation of local students by full-fee-paying foreigners adds to the confusion.

Australian tourism, meanwhile, relies on climate change–threatened natural attractions. Large domestic distances and poor infrastructure outside major centres are also problematic. In a competitive global market for visitors, Australia's position is vulnerable.

Educational services and tourism require free movement. The risk is that even when the pandemic eases, travel may not revert to its pre-COVID state. The need for vaccine passports, pre- and post-arrival testing, the availability and cost of flights and insurance, possible quarantine, and uncertain regulations, will crimp mobility.

Border closures and the loss of foreign students have exposed the higher-education sector's overinvestment, using borrowed funds, forcing institutions to retrench staff as revenues dwindled. Nor can domestic tourism fully compensate for fewer foreign visitors. Tourist operators also rely on cheap itinerant workers and young backpackers visiting Australia on a gap year or career break. During the pandemic, trapped foreigners have been denied welfare benefits and many have had to rely on charities to survive. This has all been unhelpful to virus control and has affected Australia's long-term standing as a destination for travelling workers.

Border closures have exposed the limits of using population increases to generate economic activity. In recent years, while the overall size of the Australian economy has increased, GDP per capita has stagnated. Since 2000, it has grown by less than 2 per cent per annum; over the last decade, growth has been lower. And immigration will not return to previous levels for some time. In 2021, long-term resident departures averaged around 3500 a month. Some immigrants, mostly educated professionals, left because of prolonged border closures and uncertainty over travel to visit family and friends. Others would have moved except for their family situation. This trend, if not reversed, is troubling for population growth, which also faces growing resource and infrastructure constraints, and for workforce skills.

Safe as Houses

Australian housing poses different risks. It is overvalued when evaluated against historical price-to-rent ratios

(home prices relative to annualised rent) or price-to-income ratios (house prices divided by disposable income).
Property prices can be volatile, exacerbated by the use of
borrowed money. Real estate also ties up capital, which
unlike business investments does not generate ongoing
income. It is lumpy and illiquid. Transaction costs are
high. It impedes the mobility of the workforce, with
workers unable to relocate where they cannot sell existing
houses at an acceptable price or find suitable affordable
accommodation at their destination.

At the same time, governments rely on real estate.
State governments draw around 15 per cent of revenues
from property taxes, and local governments rely almost
exclusively on this source for income. The Australian
banking system is highly exposed to the domestic housing
market. Residential mortgages constitute over 60 per cent
of total loans of Australian banks, one of the highest levels
globally and more than double that in the United States
and United Kingdom.

Household debt in Australia, primarily due to
mortgages, is currently around 130 per cent of GDP, which
is amongst the highest in the world. Household-debt-to-
disposable-income is at an all-time high of 185 per cent,
compared to 40 per cent in the 1980s. Despite record
low interest rates, around 12 per cent of income is used
to service debt, compared to 9 per cent in 1989–90
when interest rates peaked at near 17 per cent. The fear
is that rising unemployment and decreases in income
could trigger falls in real estate prices, exposing financial
system vulnerabilities.

Rising house values are masking static wages and moribund living standards, as well as exacerbating unaffordability and exaggerating inequalities. Many home buyers will never pay off their interest-only mortgages, instead effectively paying a monthly fee in perpetuity. This 'housing as a service' model is only sustainable when values are increasing and interest costs are low. The overdependence on property also means central banks cannot raise interest rates as needed to manage inflation because of the risk to house values. Real estate booms create low-quality, fictional economic growth. History shows that managing runaway property markets without a severe economic slump or financial crisis is hard.

Australia's large superannuation savings are commonly cited as evidence of the country's wealth, and it is assumed that when transferred to future generations, they will allow current high living standards to be maintained. But while providing a buffer, they are not a panacea. The size of these savings and large annual inflows (more than $100 billion) artificially elevate the values of domestic shares, real estate and privatised infrastructure assets. The system also incurs over $30 billion in annual fees and costs.

The truth is that superannuation savings may not be sufficient to meet post-work income requirements. The typical accumulated super balance at retirement age is around $200 000 for men and $110 000 for women, with the average artificially increased by a small pool of people with large balances. These amounts are well below the $600 000 to $700 000 estimated to be necessary for homeowning and debt-free couples to meet the costs of post-retirement lives, which may last twenty or more years.

The Australian Government will need to cover the shortfall in retirement savings for a large proportion of the population, and in doing so it will lose doubly. It suffers a loss of tax revenue from generous concessions (estimated at $30 billion annually and increasing), especially to wealthy individuals, and it will also bear the future cost of aged pensions and associated welfare costs. The young will have to finance payments to older generations through higher taxes or additional government debt, reduced wealth transfers from parents, and lower benefits than those awarded to their predecessors.

Remake, Remodel

Australia remains a rich country with a narrowly based economy driven by commodity exports and reliant on imports of manufactured goods. While it has some world-class industries, mainly based on natural advantages, large parts of the economy lag international competitors. It is a net importer of capital and skills, with many economic elements being outside Australia's direct control. None of these concerns about a dependence on primary industries and mining are new. The real problem is the difficulties involved in broadening Australia's economic base.

Reducing the contribution of mineral exports is nearly impossible. This was illustrated in 2021 when the rapid recovery in China and interruptions in Brazilian supply led to sharp increases in iron-ore prices. Export revenues from this single commodity rose to around 10 per cent of the Australian economy. The increase alone more than covered the pandemic losses from international students, inbound tourists and immigration. This temporarily boosted Australian incomes, until prices fell sharply in late 2021.

Australia must address some fundamental weaknesses, such as high cost structures and lagging productivity improvements. In the 2020 *Global Competitiveness Report*, released by the World Economic Forum (WEF), Australia was ranked twenty-second. In the World Bank's 'Ease of doing business' rankings, Australia placed fourteenth.

Former prime minister Paul Keating once noted that Australians were luckier than most in having been given an entire continent that was remarkably rich in minerals, but Australia persistently and egregiously wastes this wealth. In his 2010 speech 'The Challenge of Prosperity', then RBA governor Glenn Stevens used a striking analogy: in 2005, the revenue from a shipload of iron ore was sufficient to purchase 2200 flat-screen TVs; in 2010, higher prices meant this ore was worth 22 000 TVs. The equation of mineral exports and consumer electronics was unintentionally accurate: Australia has channelled its mineral wealth into consumption instead of savings, public goods, investments or a new industrial base. Much of the income has been transferred to households in the form of tax cuts and payments.

Future generations may rue the fact that the nation has repeatedly not made the most of successive mining booms.

SATYAJIT DAS

STRADDLING A BARBED-WIRE FENCE:
AUSTRALIA'S RELATIONSHIP WITH ASIA

Tension Headaches

Tensions between geography, economic interests and history complicate Australia's policy choices. Location, tectonic forces moving the continent northwards, and economic self-interest suggest an affinity with Asia, but in terms of history and culture, a majority of Australians identify with America and Europe.

The reasons are complex. Originally a British penal colony and largely populated by white Europeans following the dispossession of Indigenous peoples, Australia's links are with distant countries. Until recently, engagement with what was perceived as a backwards and poor Asia was an afterthought. Security concerns were at the forefront of this. Japan's Greater East Asia Co-Prosperity Sphere fed fear about being overwhelmed by the yellow peril. In the Cold War, this morphed into the domino theory: Australians believed that a communist takeover in one Asian nation would quickly undermine adjacent states and eventually reach the southern continent. And so Australia looked first to Britain and then, after World War II, to the United States for its defence needs.

However, over the last half-century, Asia's economic emergence and Sino-US rapprochement has driven Australian trade relationships. Prime minister Gough Whitlam's 1971 visit to, and subsequent diplomatic recognition of, China were important waypoints. But despite increasing Asian immigration and lip-service to multiculturalism, politically, socially and culturally Australia remains Western.

A key element of this is race. At the 1919 Paris Peace Conference, prime minister William Hughes voted against an amendment to the League of Nations Covenant on racial equality. Prime minister Robert Menzies, who remained in office for two decades, was allegedly reluctant to admit black countries into the British Commonwealth. The White Australia immigration policy was only ended in 1973.

Vestiges of xenophobia remain. The 2005 Cronulla riots, prime minister Tony Abbott's reintroduction in 2014 of imperial-era honours, and the episodic persecution of coloured migrants and foreign students reveal a nostalgia for the old, white, culturally homogeneous Australia. A widely read young-adults book, John Marsden's 1993 novel *Tomorrow, When the War Began*, focuses on Australian teenagers returning from a camping trip in a remote valley to find the country has been invaded by unidentified foreign forces—it speaks to particular preoccupations.

Successive Australian leaders have refused to choose between history and geography. Reconciling the political and defence partnership with the United States and economic dependence on Asia, especially China, is proving difficult. It requires, in the words of former Queensland premier Joh Bjelke-Petersen, running along a barbed-wire fence with a foot on either side.

BIG!

Asia is Australia's major trading partner, accounting for over 70 per cent of exports. In addition to minerals and agricultural products, there is inbound tourism and increasing services exports. Australians are the Filipinos of higher-end services in Asia, with expatriate doctors, pilots, lawyers and bankers fulfilling a similar function to nurses, hotel staff and domestic workers from the Philippines.

Bolstered by a 2015 free trade agreement, China dominates this trade—in Noel Coward's *Private Lives*, Elyot Chase simply and aptly describes the country as very big. China directly accounts for over 40 per cent of Australian exports. Taking into account indirect exports—sales to other countries dependent on Chinese demand—the level is actually higher. Australian exports to the United States and Europe, by contrast, are around 10 per cent. Major exports include iron ore, coal and LNG. China is the largest foreign buyer of Australian agriculture, forestry and fisheries products. Australian imports from China comprise approximately 30 per cent of the total, compared to around 20 per cent from the United States and Europe, with major items including manufactured goods, telecommunications and information technology equipment, and homewares.

China is Australia's largest source of international students. Normally, over 250 000 Chinese students are enrolled in Australian education institutions, representing 30 per cent of all international enrolments. In fact, over 80 per cent of international students are Asian.

China is also Australia's second-largest inbound tourist market (around 1.5 million arrivals) and the largest by expenditure, although tourist numbers from other Asian countries, especially India, are growing.

Chinese foreign investment in Australia is modest, under 5 per cent, lagging capital flows from North America, Europe and Japan. But despite this, it attracts significant attention because of the focus on domestically sensitive areas like mining, agriculture, infrastructure and real estate.

The correct answer to most questions about the country's recent economic prosperity is one word: China!

Sino Spat

Despite China's status as our biggest trade partner, the Sino-Australian relationship is becoming increasingly fractious.

In August 2016, the Australian Government rejected offers from the government-owned State Grid Corporation of China and Hong Kong's Cheung Kong Infrastructure to purchase major electricity assets in New South Wales, even though they offered the highest price. Australia also rejected a Chinese firm's purchase of S. Kidman & Co, a large agricultural holding, and scrutiny of Chinese purchases of real estate in Australia has increased in recent times. Concerns about Chinese ownership of energy assets and the Port of Darwin have also surfaced. In 2018, Australia banned the Chinese technology firms Huawei and ZTE from involvement in Australia's 5G network, which followed an earlier decision preventing Huawei's participation in the national broadband network.

These decisions were in part political. Some proposals were rejected on national security grounds, which conveniently meant that details could not be disclosed. In 2020 Australia passed the *Foreign Relations Act*, which allows intervention on external policy grounds in existing or proposed arrangements between Australian states and other countries. This followed the addition of a new national security test to the Foreign Investment Review Board legislation, expansion of the *Security of Critical Infrastructure Act*, and an inquiry into foreign interference in Australia's public universities and research agencies.

In no doubt about the measures' intended target, China retaliated by instituting tariffs, anti-dumping and anti-subsidy duties, and bans and restrictions on Australian imports. The affected sectors included barley, wine, cotton, timber, coal, and food products like meat and rock lobsters. Chinese foreign investment in Australia subsequently fell to the lowest level in six years. Separately, a number of Chinese Australians were detained and prosecuted for suspected espionage. Despite the restrictions, which were calibrated to minimise damage to the mainland, trade has continued at high levels, due mainly to iron-ore exports, reflecting China's need to support its aggressive infrastructure program and lack of alternative supply. But the future is fraught; for example, the return of mainland students and tourists, when borders reopen, remains uncertain.

Various considerations underlie the strained relationship. China has contributed 30–40 per cent of global economic growth since 2008, and restrictions on investment and access to resources and technology are seen as designed to prevent China's further development. Chinese leaders also bridle at criticism of their territorial claims in the South China Sea and East Asia, asserting historical legitimacy. Policies towards Taiwan and Hong Kong, both viewed as part of the mainland, are regarded as matters of sovereignty. Western concerns about human rights abuses, such as mass internments and repression in Muslim-majority Xinjiang Province, and China's overall political system, are rejected as interference in internal affairs. Claiming hypocrisy, China points to the West's poor treatment of minorities and indigenous communities and its support for murderous authoritarian regimes when convenient. Questions about the origins of COVID-19 and Chinese handling of the initial phase of the pandemic are another point of friction.

In short, Australian criticism, which follows the general Western position, is derided as slavishly adherent to the American line and a case of double standards. In November 2020, the Chinese embassy in Canberra helpfully provided Australia with a list of fourteen grievances to be addressed to improve the relationship.

Hobbesian Choices

Understanding the factors that have shaped China's rise is essential to negotiating the Sino-Australian relationship. China's growth has been similar to Germany's *Wirtschaftswunder*, Italy's *miracolo economico* and Japan's post-World War II recovery. The key elements have been low wages, high savings, investment and exports.

Under Deng Xiaoping, China converted itself into the world's factory, importing raw materials and components, then processing or assembling them for export. Improved living standards and growing urbanisation combined with foreign investment drove rapid growth. The return of a large Chinese diaspora, nicknamed *haigui* or 'sea turtles', supplied capital and skills, transforming the country. The 2008 downturn in overseas markets threatened the nation's progress, but China revived growth using massive investment programs funded by an expansion in borrowing from government-controlled banks. Since 2008, almost all of China's GDP growth has been driven by state-influenced expenditure.

In reality, Chinese economic activity may be overstated. Annual growth of say 7 per cent requires directed lending of around 15 per cent of GDP. Given that perhaps a quarter of all loans cannot be repaid, the deduction of bad debts of 4 per cent (25 per cent of the 15 per cent) equates to a more realistic 3 per cent rate of growth. Stories of wasteful, substandard Ozymandias-like projects, entire ghost cities and tens of millions of empty apartments, abound. Many will never generate adequate returns. The investment boom has created overcapacity in the steel, aluminium, cement and chemical industries.

Certainly, China's debts have become increasingly problematic. Borrowings are around 300 per cent of

GDP, an unprecedented doubling since 2008. Chinese credit intensity—the amount of debt needed to generate additional economic activity—has increased. Today, to put it in terms of dollars, between $5 and $8 of new borrowings are needed to produce $1 of activity, up from the $1 or $2 required for each dollar of growth a decade ago.

The current model, which underlies the demand for Australian exports, is fragile. Chinese leaders have repeatedly acknowledged that the country's economic foundations are unstable, unbalanced, uncoordinated and unsustainable. Policymakers recognise the need to rebalance, shifting away from debt-driven infrastructure and property investment to consumption, and moving up the value chain into technologically more advanced, higher-margin products. But legacy issues of excessive investment and over-indebtedness must first be resolved. China has successfully negotiated previous episodes of poor lending, but the current levels of debt and bad loans are much larger, the growth levels required to correct over-borrowing unattainable, and the available time shorter.

China's financial resources for managing such a transition may also be overestimated. The foreign-exchange reserves of around US$3 trillion are barely adequate when measured against the minimum requirements suggested by the International Monetary Fund, once adjustments are made for illiquid assets such as infrastructure investments, including the Belt and Road Initiative (BRI) commitments. Large investments in US Government bonds are difficult to realise because of potential falls in value and currency implications when the funds are repatriated into yuan.

With China's true budget deficit rising, its fiscal flexibility is also restricted.

The policy choices too are complex. Rebalancing the economy will lower growth and result in job losses. On the other hand, not rebalancing from investment to consumption will also result in slower growth and reduced employment. Higher consumption requires increasing household income, reducing savings or a combination of both, which means increasing wage levels and extending the rudimentary welfare system. China's health, education and pensions outlays, at around 6 per cent of GDP, are well below the 25 per cent OECD average. Increasing wages decreases competitiveness; not increasing wages increases reliance on investment, risking further malinvestment and exacerbating overcapacity.

Similarly, increasing real interest rates to compensate savers will encourage consumption but create funding problems for the financial sector, which is central to government-directed lending supporting selected firms. Tackling underperforming state-owned enterprises (SOEs) will result in bad debts and job losses, but not dealing with the sector's problems will lead to capital being tied up in unproductive industries. Recognising and writing off bad loans will potentially set off a financial crisis; however, not addressing the bank asset quality issues only delays the reckoning. Devaluing the yuan would lead to accelerated capital flight and complaints from trading partners, yet supporting the yuan reduces China's export competitiveness. Dealing with environmental issues would lead to millions of job losses, but not dealing with the problem may lead to rising health costs and ultimately millions of premature deaths. China's problems are complicated by poor demographics—its workforce will peak soon; an ageing population will retard growth.

In 2021, China instituted measures to reduce the dependence on property (20–30 per cent of GDP), reign in excessive debt and improve housing affordability. These created serious problems for real estate firms, including the Evergrande Group, which has an estimated US$300 billion worth of liabilities. As companies failed, a fear of social disorder and financial instability forced the government to intervene. With property constituting 60–75 per cent of household wealth, it protected buyers of unfinished apartments as well as suppliers, although shareholders and lenders, some of them foreigners, will ultimately suffer losses. The episode has highlighted China's complex economic challenges.

The rest of Asia shares many of China's problems. Growth is slowing, reflecting weak export markets and domestic pressures from increasing costs and the effects of rapid credit growth. Asia also faces structural problems in transiting to middle-income economies, including a lack of genuine innovation and slowing productivity improvements. Institutional weaknesses and corruption likewise persist. And while Asia has achieved important development milestones, its middle class, the coveted market for Australian products, is overstated, due to a low-income threshold for qualification. Modest incomes equivalent to US$10 000 per year, around 20 per cent of the average incomes in developed economies, limit purchasing power.

In fact, success in rebalancing Asian economies may not be to Australia's advantage. For example, if China successfully rebalances away from investment, then the demand for Australian mineral resources will diminish, although services exports may make up a part of the difference. If China is unsuccessful in doing so, then its slower growth will also reduce Australian exports. Asia's, and especially China's, feasts and famines will be shared by Australia.

Great Power Politics

Great power politics and de-globalisation provide the broader context of the Sino-Australian relationship. Central to this are tensions between China and the United States that reflect legitimate anxieties, respective strengths and weakness, domestic concerns, different perceptual frameworks, and contradictions.

China's social contract exchanges improved living standards for a Chinese Communist Party (CCP) monopoly over political power. But increasingly, slower growth is affecting real incomes and employment; for example, university graduates are finding it difficult to gain jobs consistent with their training and aspirations. To stave off the potential threat to CCP authority, China needs to become a more advanced nation, increasing earnings, especially those of low-income citizens, and providing growing opportunities for its workforce.

In response to these pressures, President Xi Jinping wants to double the economy and per-capita income by 2035. In order to meet these objectives, China must leverage its current strengths and its large domestic market, which is attractive to foreign investors. It also requires investment in research and development, and access to advanced computing, robotics, AI and life science technologies. Given the need for rapid change, this means that the CCP is reluctant to reduce its power and control over crucial economic levers, such as the SOEs and the banking sector. In turn, this makes it difficult to open up to foreigners, except on China's terms.

Unlike Western political systems, the unelected CCP's legitimacy rests on competence and self-discipline. In 2012, Xi Jinping inherited an institution widely seen as a kleptocracy that made the well-connected wealthy. To correct this, the President has instituted anti-corruption programs, some draconian, against both 'tigers and flies', and increased the emphasis on common prosperity and the rich giving back to society. The campaign threatens powerful interests who could destabilise the regime, which, while monolithic to outsiders, is riddled with significant internal factional disagreements. The success of the programs requires centralised control. Memories of the chaotic collapse of the Soviet Union also reinforce the tendency for authoritarian rule.

Xi Jinping's aggressive wolf-warrior diplomacy, a term coined from a 2017 Chinese action film, seeks to reverse China's centuries of humiliation. Reclaiming lost territory, especially Taiwan, is integral to this and President Xi's historical legacy. And China wants the West to accept its rise. Speaking at Tiananmen Square on the centenary of the creation of the CCP, China's leader pledged that any foreigner who tried to bully his country would 'dash their heads against a Great Wall of steel, forged from the flesh and blood of over 1.4 billion Chinese people'.

US policy towards China has remained consistent across presidents Obama, Trump and now Biden. Differences in rhetoric, tone and coherence notwithstanding, the object is to check China's rise. The strategy seeks to restrict the global expansion of Chinese businesses and their access to advanced technologies. It challenges China's record on human rights and political repression. China's influence in the United Nations and other multilateral institutions is confronted. In parallel, the US military has increased its battle-readiness and conducts freedom-of-navigation exercises in the South China Sea to rebut Chinese territorial claims.

There are genuine and substantial commercial issues underlying the differences, including intellectual property theft, unfair trade practices, market access, government interference in business decisions, and cyberattacks. But these are increasingly being overshadowed by the American fear of being overtaken economically and losing leadership in world affairs. Confronted with the rise of the Soviet Union in the 1950s and Japan in the 1970s and 1980s, the United States responded similarly.

America also feels betrayed, having deluded itself that engagement with China, such as supporting its accession to the World Trade Organization, would lead to domestic political changes. In later life, former US president Richard Nixon reflected that opening up to China might have been a mistake and had created a Frankenstein.

US domestic politics also affects the relationship—perceived weakness in dealings with the Middle Kingdom is electorally damaging. China fulfils the role of America's external enemy, providing a rallying point for patriots. US allies, especially Europe, are more circumspect, preferring to foster economic relationships and avoid confrontation—for most, China is a more important trading partner than America.

The risk of armed confrontation is not trivial in these circumstances. The Thucydides Trap highlights the risk of war when an emerging nation threatens an existing great power. Alternatively, it may develop from mutual national weaknesses and errors of judgement. Australia would be drawn into any conflict.

Bloc Parties

Great power rivalry feeds into de-globalisation. The United States has increasingly embraced government intervention, industrial policy and trade restrictions. It wants to secure crucial supply chains for semiconductors, batteries, rare-earth elements and vital pharmaceutical ingredients, using the justifications of national security and ensuring that jobs and production remain in America. The free movement of capital is now at risk. The United States has even threatened to cut off Chinese access to US capital markets and force the delisting of existing firms.

The world may risk retreating into political and economic isolation. The United States, the EU and China can function as closed economies. Each has a large domestic market and is largely self-sufficient in food. The United States is less exposed to trade (around 15 per cent of GDP) than other large economies, most EU trade is between its members, and China's dependence on trade is decreasing. America is also rich in natural resources, including energy; by contrast, the EU and China are net importers of energy and other raw materials. All have large and deep capital markets.

America's demographics are favourable, with its population growth higher than that of many industrialised countries which have below-replacement fertility rates. The United States and Europe are also attractive destinations for immigrants, allowing them to increase their talent pool and supplement their labour force. This shift to a closed economy is consistent with America's natural isolationism. For China, it would represent a return to traditional economic self-reliance.

A retreat from global integration presents challenges, however, for countries lacking a large domestic market or needing export markets. Strategically located nations like Switzerland and Singapore may survive as trading or financial centres. Natural-resource-rich countries like Russia and Australia will need to ally themselves with major nations and blocs, such as the United States, Europe or China, becoming preferred suppliers of food, energy or raw materials; in turn, they can reciprocate as markets for products or services and investments of their trading partners.

In any new-world order, every nation must reassess its historical ties and biases, trading off political considerations against economic prosperity and security. Australia needs to find a way to coexist with its neighbours, especially the Middle Kingdom.

Carpetbaggers

Australian involvement with Asia, especially China as the dominant regional power, is best described as shallow. The general population is wary: for most, Asia is merely a cheap, exotic holiday destination and a source of culinary variety. Australian businesses, outside of exporters, are domestically oriented. In a *Sydney Morning Herald* cartoon, a teacher tells her students: 'Children, the Asian century is upon us. We need to ENGAGE with Asia so we can PROFIT from their rising middle class.' Asians, meanwhile, regard Australians as carpetbaggers, a people seeking to ally themselves with a region with which they have no real connection, for economic gain.

Australians have an ever-present tendency to revert to the comfort of the Anglosphere. In September 2021, Australia entered into an arrangement with the United States and United Kingdom (AUKUS) to acquire nuclear-powered submarines. Justified on changing security priorities, the choice allowed enhanced military coordination with the Americans. But viewed against the background of a growing US military presence in Australia, the Five Eyes intelligence alliance and the Quad (US, India, Japan and Australia) strategic dialogue, the decision clearly reflected concerns about China.

In fact, AUKUS antagonised both allies and foes. France took umbrage at the cancellation of its own contract to sell conventionally powered submarines and a duplicitous lack of consultation. The EU, with whom Australia was in discussions about a free-trade agreement, expressed solidarity with the French. Regional neighbours believed it demonstrated Australia's unconvincing commitment towards Asia. They feared the decision undermined local stability and international non-proliferation efforts as well as intensifying an arms race. China saw it as provocative, confirming Australia's status as an American vassal state.

In the end, this expensive high-end vanity purchase, which enjoyed popular support, has made Australia less secure and less autonomous. A reliance for protection on the United States, with its growing economic weakness, narrow 'America First' national interest, increasingly unpredictable leadership and history of abandoning allies, may prove as illusory as Australia's earlier dependence on Britain. At the AUKUS announcement, President Biden, a weak transitional figure, couldn't even remember the Australian Prime Minister's name, referring to him as 'the fella from down under'.

Australia cannot economically replace China. Beyond trade, cooperation is essential for managing security issues such as refugees, illegal immigration and climate change. China's influence over not just Asia but the world's economic and commercial architecture is con- siderable and growing. Neither America nor its allies have matched China's BRI spending on other countries' infrastructure or pandemic assistance. Nor should China's ability to punish or reward its trading partners be underestimated. Taking sides in the Sino-US contest, a struggle which may define the twenty-first century, will come at a price.

For nineteenth-century British statesman Lord Palmerston, countries did not have eternal allies or perpetual enemies, just permanent interests. Europe sustains commercial links with China despite political differences. South-East Asian countries maintain concurrent relationships with America and China. Assuming an unwillingness to acquire a nuclear deterrent, Swiss-like neutrality in international affairs is an underrated alternative. On human rights and political dogma, it is simply beyond Australian capabilities to right all the painful and dangerous wrongs that exist in this world.

IDEOLOGICAL NECROPHILIA: AUSTRALIA'S POLICY PUZZLES

Lazy Policy

Australian policymakers, alongside global contemporaries, are obsessed with 'ideological necrophilia', Venezuelan journalist Moisés Naím's term for ideas tried but found wanting.

A central belief is market-driven solutions. Its re-emergence amidst the economic stagnation of the 1970s reflected failures of the mixed and central planned economy models. But markets are imperfect. Lack of competition, entry and exit barriers, limited buyers and sellers, incomplete information and irrational behaviour prevent efficient resource allocation. There is the tragedy of the commons: independent, self-interested actors over-exploit the resources available to all, such as drinkable water and breathable air, to the detriment of everybody. There is the free-rider problem: the use of a shared public commodity by people without payment. There are externalities: the uncompensated costs or benefits of economic activity imposed on others.

The pandemic, according to free marketeers, demonstrated the superiority of private enterprise, which developed vaccines that brought the virus under control. In fact, governments spent billions to finance, coordinate and make advance purchases to correct a market failure. Large private pharmaceutical companies had previously ignored coronavirus vaccines because of the associated costs, risks and inadequate financial returns. No wonder John Kenneth Galbraith thought free-market advocate Milton Freidman's misfortune was that his theories had been tried!

The lazy reliance on markets is driven by practicalities. Responsibility is devolved to unelected functionaries. Politicians can blame others or claim credit after outcomes are apparent, whilst avoiding difficult choices. Unfortunately, these technocrats lack the appetite, skills and experience for deep-seated structural reforms, which are glibly dismissed as Soviet-style *Gosplans* that would interfere in market mechanisms. Instead, they rely on what they know—monetary and fiscal tricks.

Economic Fetishes

Encouraged by US Federal Reserve chairmen Paul Volcker and Alan Greenspan's success in reducing inflation and managing serial financial crises, interest rates became an essential policy instrument. QE performed a similar function—where interest rates are zero and the price of money cannot be decreased, supply is increased. It lowered long-term interest rates and financed government spending.

Lower financing costs are meant to encourage borrowing, consumption and investment. But in practice it may not work, especially where rates are very low. Falling income on savings forces greater thrift, reducing consumption and demand. The lower cost of capital encourages automation, reducing employment. Under a regime of very low rates, investors purchase shares in search of income, and companies then must finance dividends by shedding workers and reducing investment. Low rates do not necessarily increase the supply of credit, as banks may be reluctant to lend. Borrowers only take on debt based on need, capacity and confidence in their future prospects.

Low interest rates cause asset price bubbles and, ultimately, financial instability. Since 2008, they have driven up property prices, reducing affordability and leading to higher mortgage debt. Cutting rates increased the cost of existing houses, rather than expanding the construction of new dwellings. Most credit now finances purchases of existing assets rather than new capital investment.

In reality, low rates mainly support asset prices which secure high debt levels. Reducing servicing costs makes the otherwise unmanageable borrowings manageable.

Fiscal policy can increase aggregate demand, relying on a multiplier effect where each dollar spent creates more than that in new economic activity. But again, in practice, the multiplicative effects are uncertain. If spending finances consumption, then it needs to be ongoing. If financing investment, then the project should generate an adequate financial or social return. John Maynard Keynes's plan for workers to dig holes and then fill them in provides employment but uncertain long-term benefits.

Fiscal programs are often poorly directed. Australia's 2009 home insulation (Pink Batts) program was riddled with problems. The government's digital broadband network was late, overbudget and technologically deficient, lagging many Asian countries in performance.

The Australian dollar has increasingly become an important tool for discretely adjusting purchasing power. Low interest rates and QE are used to manage the currency. After the 2001 dotcom bubble collapsed, the RBA engineered a devaluation to around US$0.48. After the GFC, the value fell to US$0.64. In March 2020, as the pandemic hit, the Australian dollar declined to US$0.61.

In theory, devaluation lowers the cost of Australian products for foreigners. But demand for mining and agricultural products are not price-elastic. Australia must capture market share from competitors. With most commodities priced in US$, a weaker Australian dollar is irrelevant. Non-cost factors are important in purchasing decisions concerning tourism, education and medical services. As Australia imports most manufactured goods, devaluation results in higher local prices, effectively reducing living standards. Further, Australia is a capital importer which finances itself primarily in its own currency, and falls in the dollar's value result in overseas investors suffering losses, unless hedged. The risk makes the country a less attractive investment destination.

Ultimately, a policy of devaluation is futile when all major nations have similar policies. Everybody cannot, by definition, have the cheapest currency.

Financial measures are temporary expedients, short-term relief purchased at great cost. And with rates at zero or even negative, and with abundant liquidity and government debt levels high, traditional policies are reaching their operating limits. But repeated use makes them difficult to withdraw. For example, normalising interest rates is difficult because of unsustainably high borrowings and irrational asset prices. In an addicted world, bad news is now perversely good news for prices of shares and houses as it presages ever-lower rates and more stimulus.

Adopting a path-of-least-regret, officials simply pursue policies that they admit may not be effective.

Money for All

Facing problems resistant to conventional solutions, policymakers have embraced modern monetary theory (MMT), which conveniently sidesteps normal boundaries.

It is a sophisticated version of US vice-president Dick Cheney's 'deficits don't matter' argument.

A state, MMT argues, finances spending by creating money, not by taxes or borrowing. Where it can print its currency, a country can run deficits and accumulate debt with few limits. The theory is a melange of old ideas. Keynesian deficit spending has been used since the 1930s. A country's ability to print its own currency has been accepted since the gold standard ended in 1971. Central bank–financed government spending via QE is now standard.

Under MMT, wherever demand is inadequate, governments must spend to move the economy to full employment. This is done via a jobs guarantee for everyone willing to work. An alternative, rejected by MMT purists, is a government-funded universal basic income (UBI). The politically attractive UBI, an unconditional flat-rate payment to every citizen, funded by MMT, may address poverty traps inherent in welfare systems. It could alleviate labour's declining share of income and the loss of jobs from automation. It may improve government-assistance programs by minimising bureaucracy, delivery costs and political exploitation or benefit fraud.

Small-scale trials of UBI in a number of countries have been inconclusive—its full economic and social impact, especially on work incentives, remains controversial. What is known is that MMT ignores several issues.

The source of useful, well-compensated jobs is unclear. The impact of employment-reducing technology and competitive global supply chains is glossed over. It is also unclear whether the deficit spending needs to be productive. An old communist-era joke states that in the Soviet Union workers pretended to work while the state pretended to pay them.

Large deficits financed by money creation might lead to inflationary pressures. MMT advocates argue that the risk of higher prices only exists if the economy is at full employment or there are capacity shortages. But fear of inflation or loose fiscal policy may create volatility in the prices of real assets like property and commodities, including food and other essentials, with profound social implications.

As Australia borrows in its own currency, foreign investors must have confidence in the stability of the exchange rate. If financial markets lose confidence, then a devaluation of the Australian dollar, even rendering the currency worthless or unacceptable, is possible. Businesses would be unable to import goods or only at very high costs. The expense of servicing foreign currency–denominated debt would rise sharply.

As a sovereign with its own fiat currency, Australia could adopt MMT. But private businesses or households cannot print money. As the majority of Australian debt is non-governmental, the state might have to assume private debt.

To implement MMT, policymakers must define the full employment rate or the UBI level and structure. Accurate, unambiguous and timely information on unemployment, inflation, money supply statistics or output gaps must be available. Introducing MMT may create an exchange rate or inflation shock that destabilises existing investments and trade. And once set in motion, it may not be controllable. It is uncertain what would happen if MMT failed—as the early twentieth-century Weimar Republic illustrated, the road back from any experiment is painful.

MMT may also make citizens wary. Instead of spending the money received, they may question a world where governments give cash away. In the extreme case, as the prices of gold and cryptocurrencies highlight, the population may simply stop trusting or using the currency.

MMT is now being implemented by stealth. Emergency pandemic income support measures, especially the one-off payments and increases in welfare entitlements, may foreshadow more permanent arrangements. But the debt will have to be paid for by future taxes. Alternatively, government stimulus may create inflation, an implicit tax, reducing household and business purchasing power. Money creation to finance governments cannot avoid normal financial constraints. Something for nothing is understandably attractive, but it is also unrealistic.

Overdue Weeding

The alternative to tangled macro-economic monetary finance is micro-economic or structural reform. There, the focus is on correcting market failures to increase competitiveness and flexibility by reforming the workforce, cost structures and social policy. There is no shortage of challenges.

Australia's demographic transition means that by 2060, over 23 per cent of the population will be over sixty-five, a rise of around 7 per cent from the current-day level.

The ratio of working-age people to those over sixty-five will fall from 4.0 to 2.7 over the next forty years; it was 6.6 in 1982. Higher birth rates—one for each parent and one for the country—is an option, but China's difficulties in shifting from its one-child policy shows the practical problems of population engineering.

Given the Australian continent's limited ability to support more people, increasing workforce participation has advantages. Enabling child-bearing women and older people to work more easily and for longer would help address the dependency ratio. Flexible immigration, including short-term guest workers who can return to their homes with a substantial nest egg, is another option. Better use of immigrant skills would help, too. Many new arrivals are forced to work menial jobs due to lack of recognition of their qualifications under unreasonably restrictive trade practices.

Australian labour market reform currently concentrates on flexible work arrangements, reduced union membership, and moving from collective to individual bargaining. The aim is to reduce wages and benefits. Yet Germany, with high wages and strong unions, demonstrates that competitiveness does not simply mean low labour costs.

The quality of human capital is important. The quality of education in Australia has declined. The country ranks behind Northern Europe and North and East Asia in literacy, mathematics and science. Governments, teachers and parents blame each other for the deterioration. Curriculums have shifted from hard knowledge to cultural values. Assessment systems are weak. The COVID-19 pandemic revealed that school, for many families, is primarily a free child-minding service.

Australia's poor workforce planning creates mismatches between graduates and skills needs. Some European countries stream youth from an early age, depending on natural attributes and interest. They follow different training pathways to ensure employability, and skilled trades enjoy a status comparable to professions. Australia's 'anyone can be anything' ethos is unrealistic.

University education produces qualifications of questionable utility and is unnecessary for many jobs. It must be balanced by technical training. Recent initiatives to resuscitate Australia's TAFE system to improve vocational education may address this need, reversing years of neglect.

Technological unemployment will require lifelong retraining to facilitate job mobility. Many workers will not reinvent themselves as knowledge workers, so strategies for unemployable workers are needed.

Australia's productivity growth, outside of the mining sector, has declined noticeably since the 1990s. It reflects the shift to services, such as health and aged care, which are labour-intensive and involve complex, non-repetitive tasks. Other influences include lack of investment, a reluctance to adopt new technologies, and slower skill improvements. Monetary finance has slowed the reallocation of capital from inefficient industries, retarding Schumpeterian creative destruction. Australia has few strategies to improve productivity, other than greater digitalisation.

Australia's infrastructure is ageing and needs renewal. Recent spending on transport and telecommunications has been well overdue. Energy policy remains confused, due to ideological differences around renewables and climate. The nation, a major energy exporter, faces gas shortages and high electricity costs. With many Australian industries being oligopolies, better enforcement of trade practices legislation would improve competition, lowering costs and creating better products.

There is scope for the deregulation of professions. Archaic practices lower efficiency, and entry barriers, which create artificial shortages, need to be changed. Allowing paramedics, nurses and pharmacists to provide some medical services, for example, would lower presently high health costs. Uniform Australia-wide licensing, merging different functions and simplifying proceedings, would similarly reduce the cost of legal services.

According to WEF rankings, Australian businesses face a high regulatory burden. This is because many rules do not serve their intended purpose, and new laws frequently respond to vocal constituencies and skilfully marshalled media advocates. The cost often outweighs benefits. Compliance, now a large industry, focuses on ticking boxes to avoid legal liability rather than promoting higher standards. Poor enforcement makes even necessary regulation ineffective. One example is the unsatisfactory supervision and certification of construction, which leaves home purchasers exposed to large rectification costs.

Australia's overall taxation levels, at 28 per cent of GDP, are not high amongst its peers. But the tax system is overly complex. The related legislation runs to tens of thousands of pages, necessitating expensive tax advisers. The tax base is also narrow, heavily dependent on personal income taxes. The goods and services tax (GST) base is eroding. Fuel excise will be affected by vehicle electrification. Property taxes and mineral royalties are volatile. Expensive tax concessions for extractive industries, dividends, capital gains, superannuation and property ownership are distortionary. Anomalies abound.

Tax reform has become synonymous with lower rates. Politically popular personal income tax cuts merely reverse bracket creep, where people's rising nominal incomes make them subject to higher marginal tax rates. The simple answer—indexing scales to inflation—is resisted, as it would deprive the government of billions in additional annual tax revenue that accrues by default.

Greater taxation of consumption, property and resources will be required. The rate and coverage of the GST needs amendment. As at March 2021, household wealth in Australia was $12.7 trillion, an increase of $1.7 trillion over the preceding twelve months. These are mainly capital gains on property and financial investments, some held in superannuation schemes. Extending tax coverage to include wealth and estates is one option, albeit an electorally unpopular one. Another is the politically taboo subject of taxing residences.

Tax avoidance is a favourite Australian sport. Many sympathise with the late businessman Kerry Packer, who refused to pay taxes because he disagreed with how the government spent them. One option is a principle-based rather than a detailed rule-based system and the ability to retrospectively prosecute taxpayers who ignore the legislative intent. This would reduce the scope of exploitative tax planning. The 2010 Australia's Future Tax System Review identified 138 areas for reform, but few of these recommendations have been implemented.

There are also irregularities in the welfare system. More rigorous means testing, co-payments for some services and plugging loopholes would allow better targeting of intended recipients. Addressing inequality would boost the workforce and productivity—simply ensuring that women's salaries were the same as men's, for example, would boost consumption.

Since the deregulation of the 1980s, the introduction of the GST and some labour market changes, Australian structural reform has stalled. There is no shortage of ideas, just a gridlocked system lacking agreement on even modest transformations.

Grand Designs

Some believe that Australia needs an industrial policy, an official strategic plan for the economy. In fact, there have been many, including the 'Asian Century Strategy', the 'Dining Boom' (a shift to become Asia's food bowl) and the often reprised 'Clever Country' or 'Knowledge Economy' (emphasising skills and innovation). These policies have inevitably lacked detail but espouse the same ideal. Australia's knowledge-based economy would leverage expertise, research and intellectual property to create advanced, world-beating industries in technology, life sciences, media, education and financial services.

Some proposals would combine Australian resource wealth and new technologies. The focus is on the minerals needed for the transition away from fossil fuels, which would be processed using emissions-free energy and hence regenerate manufacturing. But new mining ventures, such as lithium, may strain limited water supplies. Downstream processing, such as aluminium smelting, has been tried before with variable results. Some new technologies, such as carbon sequestration and green hydrogen, are unproven at industrial scale.

In any case, concrete actions rarely extend beyond advertising the initiative and the associated funding and incentives. Tax and financing inducements generally attract astute businesses, often foreign, with no guarantee that they will continue local operations if the benefits are removed. And strategies, especially around innovation, have indeterminate outcomes. Genius cannot be engineered on demand. Selecting national champions is error-prone. Even if successful, Australia may not capture the benefits. Business will migrate to locations with attractive finance, cost and tax structures, and proximity to major customers and workforces. Many promising Australian firms have moved overseas or been bought by foreign interests. Public investment may not generate returns for the sponsoring nation.

While some innovations will prove significant, their overall impact may be limited. While a few creators capture large benefits, innovation now has a limited effect on economic growth. Unlike pivotal nineteenth-century inventions, few modern technologies have created entirely new large-scale industries which increase employment and income levels. In fact, innovation today mostly replaces labour with capital, reducing skill requirements, employment and wages.

Techno-nationalism is not necessarily synonymous with strong economic growth. Innovative economies are not always the most successful. Even in the United States, the sector remains around 10 per cent of total output and private employment. Technology workers, defined broadly, make up around 8 per cent of the overall US workforce. Less than 1 per cent are employed in industries that did not exist in 2000.

Politicians and policymakers, struggling with their smartphones and lacking basic digital competence, now see salvation in technology. Free-market advocates plead for public financing and assistance for innovation once seen as the inevitable outcome of competitive forces. Shrewd entrepreneurs and their supporting cast of consultants, lawyers and lobbyists exploit the opportunity gleefully.

Inescapable Realities

Asked where growth comes from, Glenn Stevens once suggested that most of the time it simply comes from known areas and new things. This inherently optimistic Micawber-like strategy may be a realistic option. Australia may be best served by structural reforms that foster a healthy, skilled workforce, and cost structures which can be the foundation of a productive, competitive economy. Longer-term initiatives, such as funding of basic research, improving education, promoting science and ensuring high quality infrastructure, may produce the best results. And it would be best to avoid frequent changes and let the strategy play out. The coordination of key elements, aligning trade policy, foreign affairs and industrial planning, is essential.

Of course, no plan can guarantee success. Fierce competition from other nations, with similar strategies and objectives, is constant. There is a need to be opportunistic, with the current pandemic, de-globalisation and geopolitics allowing the reshoring of strategically important industries, much as the United States and others are doing. The approach requires German sociologist Max Weber's 'slow boring of hard boards'. This conflicts with short political time horizons and a constant hunger for media minutes. It exceeds the attention span of the modern, Marvel superhero, all-action policymaker.

Reform does not guarantee that living standards can be maintained. Change does not mean that Australia's prospects will get better. But unless essential changes are made, they will not improve.

NOTHING TO SEE HERE: AUSTRALIA'S POLITICAL AND CIVIC DISENGAGEMENT

An Irrelevant Election

Political leadership backed by popular support is a precondition for action. The 2019 federal election provided an insight into Australia's willingness to change. Instead of the usual focus on living standards, grand spending promises, border security, immigration and cultural identity, that election turned, in part, on tax minutiae.

One issue was the refund of dividend tax credits. Changes in 2001 led to widespread abuse and tax minimisation, benefiting large self-managed superannuation funds. The Australian Labor Party (ALP) proposed reversing the changes, saving $59 billion over the medium term. The second concerned negative gearing, where individuals invest in property using borrowed money— the interest expense reduces the income tax payable while the capital gain on the asset is taxed at a concessional rate. The budgetary cost was over $10 billion annually, so the ALP proposed limiting the practice. The Liberal and National Party coalition (LNP) opposed both proposals, helping secure a narrow victory.

It was nothing new. Australia's GST took decades of dithering. The original proponent, treasurer Paul Keating, was overruled by prime minister Robert Hawke. Later, after becoming prime minister himself, Keating opposed the GST, securing an election victory when Opposition leader John Hewson couldn't explain the tax on a birthday cake. Finally, prime minister John Howard introduced the tax after earlier stating that he wouldn't.

This episode highlights the problems of modern policymaking. Electors are unwilling to support reforms where there is an associated personal cost or disadvantage. Learning from its 2019 failure, the ALP has discarded the controversial tax changes, shifting away from substantive policies.

It also illustrates that politics is no longer a contest of ideas. Elections are a succession of negative campaigns highlighting the other side's failings whilst trumpeting character and personal appeal. The legitimacy of, and trust in, politicians, policymakers, institutions and processes has been lost.

The Economy, Stupid!

Liberal democracies are not the best form of government, simply, as Winston Churchill observed, less bad than other forms. It requires prosperity. James Carville's advice to president Bill Clinton was succinct: 'It's the economy, stupid!'

A growing economy allows the bounty to be divided. Taxes are cut, public money is sprayed around. But economic problems, escalating resource scarcity and accelerating environmental threats loom large. Slower and brittle future growth means that living standards may stagnate or even decline. Over time, the social contract has evolved beyond security, property rights, access to justice and political participation. Australians now expect generous entitlements, including education, health care, housing, transport, social safety nets and retirement benefits. The ability of the state to meet these growing commitments is now in doubt. The time of inexhaustible plenitude may be past.

New Politics

In Australia, for a long time, the political system was a comfortable sharing arrangement between the conservative right and more progressive left. They competed, with government changing periodically. But this modus vivendi is now unworkable.

An essential issue is the challenge of differentiating political brands. With all sides accepting free markets and economic rationalism, the differences are marginal. Conservatives advocate smaller government, lower taxes and personal freedoms, while progressive forces want greater redistribution of wealth and stronger welfare systems.

There has also been a shift in support bases. Conservative forces traditionally relied on the wealthy, business interests, professionals and libertarians; progressive elements depended on workers, the disadvantaged, and people seeking reformation of the system. But changing economic structures have undermined support for the left. Globalisation and the decline of manufacturing have damaged the living standards and prospects of workers, with a parallel fall in union support and the emergence of small individual self-employers. Left-leaning urban progressives are absorbed by environmental, conservation and social issues, where their views differ from those of many traditional ALP voters. Support for the LNP has split to a lesser extent, with more ideologically extreme right-wing members rejecting the drift to the political centre.

This has subtly shifted the battlelines. Politicians now eschew the economy, environment and international relations, focusing instead on the culture wars, with their emphasis on values, morality and lifestyle. Recent Australian political discourse has been dominated by gender and sexuality, history, Indigenous rights, immigration, multiculturalism, domestic violence and the monarchy. While worthy, the issues themselves lead to intellectual dead ends but create useful cleavages of opinion. Politicians can exploit societal disagreement and polarisation, with the right railing against political correctness and the left objecting to political incorrectness. Even the pandemic can be politicised—lockdowns, social distancing and masking or vaccination mandates become issues of personal choice and freedom.

Both parties profess to counter the influence of insiders and increase accountability. The irony of the privileged attacking elites of which they are a part has gone unacknowledged. With election results turning on a modest number of votes in a few marginal electorates, the parties now compete on their legitimacy to represent specific interests or constituencies.

Conservatives, now recast as the party of the disenfranchised, appeal to traditionally left-leaning workers, small business owners and the poor. Copying Richard Nixon's appeal to the 'silent majority', the LNP seeks the support of 'battlers' and 'mum and dad Australians'. The ALP is portrayed as an agency for 'bleeding heart' urban elites, forced to defend itself against suggestions of having betrayed its true followers and being soft on immigration, security and social matters.

Politicians rearrange old hatreds: young versus old, country versus city, prosperous versus impoverished, one tribe against another. They exploit prejudices, conscious and unconscious, by playing up small differences and tangles, with wedge issues helping to split demographic or population groups. They triangulate, presenting topics as above politics, thereby gaining credit for adopting their opponent's policies, which protects against attacks on that issue.

There is no strategy, simply tactics. It is not an ideal framework for dealing with the complex issues that confront Australia.

Media–Political Complex

The failures are attributed to professional politicians, presidential-style politics, poll and focus group–driven leadership, short electoral cycles and 24/7 media scrutiny.

Arguably, politicians aren't professional enough. The typical path is university politics followed by work in the policy establishment, unions or in a politician's office. It helps to be part of a political dynasty, or you can buy your way in. Few have substantive real-world experience; most are illiterate on key matters. Mediocrity or failure is not an obstacle.

Media coverage heavily influences politics. Every utterance and gesture is parsed to death. Volume masks a lack of quality. A reporter's longevity, coveted columnist status and book deals require maintaining access. Reporting becomes the recitation of press releases, fawning exclusives and occasional gossipy inside stories or hatchet jobs, laden with tabloid plots of ambition, betrayal, scandal and malfeasance.

Coteries of politicians, apparatchiks and reporters now form a parallel universe of interest primarily to each other and political addicts. It is irrelevant to ordinary people focused on routine survival. For most voters, it amounts to a few seconds of the choreographed drama of parliamentary question time and press briefings. Politics is something most think about when an election is called. Electors see political operatives as grasping and untrustworthy, those who go to Canberra to do good and stay to do well.

Voter suppression, gerrymandering and control of information have reduced the value of suffrage. Ballot papers feature bloviating candidates selected by a small number of party members via an opaque process. Citizens must then select between the catastrophic and the unpalatable. The most popular contender is 'none of the above'. Faced with a choice between an ineffectual middle, the utopian left and fundamentalist right, voter participation, where not mandatory, has steadily declined.

Politics has degenerated into scripted entertainment, filled with the tropes of docudramas and reality shows. US president Trump's political success was based on his celebrity as a TV star on *The Apprentice*. UK prime minister Boris Johnson also benefited from a successful career in the public eye.

All of this means that political reform may be harder than reshaping economic policy or international relationships. Perhaps Australians should consider Douglas Adams's advice in *The Hitchhiker's Guide to the Galaxy*: find the person who least wants the job and therefore can be relied upon to do it in the most detached and parsimonious manner possible.

Democratic Suicide

Australia's political system and an unrelenting degradation of institutions is increasingly unconducive to progress. Prime minister Paul Keating thought leadership was 'being right and being strong', not 'whether you go through some shopping centres, tripping over TV crews' cords'. Today's aspirants believe that leading requires following and then getting out in front of the crowd.

Policies are reactive, transactional, short-term and inconsistent. Perennial favourites include cake-ism, the notion that it is possible to simultaneously consume and keep the confectionary; another is boosterism, or spending sprees to buy voters. This is governing without making hard choices. Anything difficult is deflected. Recent and expensive royal commissions on aged care, disability, natural disaster arrangements, child sexual abuse, the detention of Indigenous children, veteran suicides, trade unions and banking misconduct—which may soon be joined by a royal commission into the handling of the pandemic—have been show trials that propose already recognised remedies. The recommendations are dutifully accepted but never fully implemented.

Yes Minister's Sir Humphrey Appleby maintained that a strong public service provides stability, continuity, pursuance of long-term objectives and accountability. Indeed, Menzies placed more faith in his departmental heads—the 'Seven Dwarfs'—than in his lightweight ministers. But the public service has been politicised where senior positions are political gifts. Incumbents face guilt by association with previous governments and are purged, as in John Howard and Tony Abbott's 1996 and 2013 nights of the long knives.

External appointments can bring expertise and an outside perspective, but they can also bring slavish and uncritical compliance. Meretricious outsiders are frequently part of complex patronage systems, focused on career advancement or future assignments. Performance measurement, beloved of management consultants, is difficult for the provision of public services. Consultant fees, now collectively running into billions of dollars, outweigh cost savings from public service reductions.

In reality, governments can no longer govern. Elected bodies display Lenin's 'parliamentary cretinism'. Public institutions now lack the quality, skills, organisational memory and courage to deliver the required evidence-based, non-partisan policy choices.

Legislation serves specific interests. Partisan think tanks and policy forums masquerade as thought leaders while proselyting for their pay masters. American economist Mancur Olson, in *The Logic of Collective Action* and *The Rise and Decline of Nations*, argued that coalitions form over time in democratic societies and market economies. Intensive, well-funded lobbying influences policies, benefiting narrow interest groups and leaving large costs to be borne by the rest of the population. The system becomes paralysed, causing inevitable and irretrievable economic decline.

Since 2007, Australia, once noted for its somnolent politics, has had six prime ministers compared to four in the previous thirty-two years. Few have served a full term. *The Economist*, for one, has questioned how Australia has been served by serial political assassinations. Current Prime Minister Scott Morrison's path to power was his accomplished navigation of the Liberal Party's internal wars. His forte is reductive formulaic advertising slogans: 'Stop the boats', 'Jobs and growth', 'The virus makes the rules', 'The gold standard', 'Technology, not taxes'. Dull, inadequate leadership dooms decisive action on critical issues, further reducing faith in government.

The inertia will only worsen, partly because most alternatives to the fractured political apparatus are unappealing. In many countries, voters seeking certainty and simple solutions have turned to populist authoritarian leaders. Rejecting spin-driven policy vacuums, they fall in behind messianic, fairy-floss-promising charlatans. Prime minister Tony Abbott's reign was an experiment in such strong-man politics. Another possibility is ungovernability, with the 6 January 2021 storming of the US Capitol in Washington and persistent partisan deadlock evidencing America's transformation into a failed First World state—Somalia with nukes.

US founding father John Adams thought that democracy was not long-lasting, that without the right conditions, it wastes, exhausts and murders itself.

Ghosts of Federation

Australia's political structure is also increasingly unfit for purpose. Major parties' share of the vote is falling.

Independent candidates, as well as smaller parties, are gaining traction—they now play the role of political kingmakers or shape the political agenda. In Australia's bicameral parliamentary system, governments find themselves mostly impotent, without the necessary support in both houses to pass anything other than anodyne legislation.

Australia is also eight separate principalities united by mutual loathing. The differences between individual states and territories create imbalances. Mining activity is concentrated in Western Australia and Queensland, while New South Wales and Victoria rely on services, tourism and construction. There are differences in social attitudes: as political scientist Seymour Martin Lipset observed, 'every country has a South'.

The pandemic has laid bare the deficiencies within the Federation. Disagreements over health policy and state border closures may presage more-difficult-to-bridge schisms, severely hampering the ability to address major policy issues in a unified manner. Yet eliminating one layer of government, reallocating powers and major constitutional changes are a fantasy. To paraphrase Upton Sinclair, politicians and policy mavens will not alter something when their power, status and salary depends on doing the opposite.

Beyond the Seas

External dimensions inform issues like the environment, resource security, economic management, defence, illegal immigration and refugees. Solutions require international cooperation, but domestic political considerations increasingly dominate Australia's foreign relations, especially with Asia.

Illegal immigration, partially the result of Australia's destabilising Middle East and Afghanistan interventions alongside Western partners, is one example. In violation of international treaty obligations, Australian policy—popular with most voters—requires turning back refugee boats, with potentially fatal consequences. Arrivals are incarcerated and processed offshore; they cannot enter Australia even if they have legitimate asylum or humanitarian claims. Australia has paid Cambodia, Papua New Guinea and Nauru to host processing centres and accept asylum seekers, actions that transfer the problem to poorer neighbours and remain a source of friction.

Australia has also reduced foreign aid funding by a quarter in real terms since 2013. During the pandemic, Australian support of embattled regional countries was small compared to that offered by China. Australia's ability to engage in multinational efforts on issues such as climate change is similarly uncertain. Wedged by consumer anger at electricity costs, risks to living standards and its large fossil fuel industry (Prime Minister Morrison once praised a lump of coal in parliament), the nation is deeply divided on environmental issues.

Keep the Change!

Australians lack an appetite for fundamental change. Ever-rising prosperity has created an individualistic culture, a

'Me' rather than a 'We' society. This is why many considered the public health response to COVID-19 an infringement of personal liberty. Anger and resistance increased as the pandemic continued, with growing non-compliance.

Expectations are high. In an entitled 'What I want, when I want it, where I want it' world, forfeiting anything for the common good is unpopular. Those 'with' do not want to lose what they have. Those 'without' do not have anything to give up. The early and shallow 'We are all in this together' solidarity of the pandemic dissipated quickly as threats to individual health and wealth escalated.

Even before the virus, most Australians, especially in urban areas, lived in splendid self-isolation. Interactions are primarily within compact and like-minded circles of family, friends and work acquaintances. There is a decline in political and civic engagement. Community means personal interests, leisure activities or issues directly impacting individuals, with opposition to anything that affects amenities. The visceral threat of COVID-19 intensified the self-absorption.

Despite the abundance of available news and information, people are poorly informed. Democracy's failures lie, in part, in the electorate's meagre understanding of issues—Churchill allegedly thought that the best argument against democracy was a five-minute conversation with the average voter. One problem is informational quality. The waning of conventional media has caused a decline in trusted, verified and edited content. Constant streamed news places a premium on sensational and attention-grabbing clickbait rather than on facts and thoughtful analysis. The real problem, however, is confirmation bias. People seek out views that coincide with their own. Social media and the Internet allow people to filter out what they do not want to hear. A decline in critical thinking limits discrimination between information and misinformation.

An ideas industry of self-promoting talking heads, eager to sell themselves or their products, compounds the problem. Celebrity influencers and true authorities are indistinguishable. Nassim Nicholas Taleb labelled them 'intellectual idiots'. This inner circle of semi-erudite experts on being an expert crowds the airwaves, providing opinions on everything. It fosters confusion and mistrust. People retreat to impressions and opinions of people like them, amplifying the echo chamber effect. The pandemic revealed the consequences: many people dismissed the virus's existence or refused vaccinations on spurious grounds.

There is limited tolerance of risk. Unexposed to wars, untimely death or hardships, most people assume that bad things cannot happen to them. So when terrorism, financial crises, extreme weather events, an influx of refugees and the pandemic create anxiety, people demand that the government shield them and their lifestyles, irrespective of the cost.

Evolutionary biologist Peter Turchin argues that Western society overproduces overeducated elites who are underemployed or otherwise denied the status that they were led to expect. Forced increasingly to retreat to the hotel of mum and dad by unaffordable housing, this younger cohort faces falling living standards, environmental problems, declining public services and moribund politics. The pandemic, with its interrupted education, diminishing job prospects and insecure futures, has only heightened the disillusionment, sharpening intergenerational strains. The system now only works for some, not everyone.

In physics, entropy, a measure of a system's disorder, increases with the passage of time. In many countries, the state's poor handling of the pandemic has prompted unrest and dissent. The backdraft from policymakers and would-be-martinets' inept handling of multiple crises is unpredictable. The society we live in is our creation. The current trajectory, reminiscent of the 1920s and 1930s, ends in instability.

WHAT IS TO BE DONE?

The COVID-19 pandemic has revealed the economic, political and social cul-de-sac that Australia finds itself in. Facing intractable multiple crises and unpalatable solutions, government and citizenry have retreated to plausible deniability. Cognitive dissonance is a religion, deflection an art form. Underlying the lack of action is disavowal. Socially organised denial means that abstract knowledge is disconnected from political, social and private life.

Humans may be poorly equipped to deal with complex, large, long-term, slow-acting and universal problems. They find it difficult to balance short-term losses of personal wealth and lifestyle against long-term nebulous benefits. They do not equate personal choices with invisible benefits for others, sometimes in faraway lands. Hardwired to indecision when confronted with massive problems, humans reject uncomfortable facts and escape into hope.

Many adopt a quasi-religious belief in technology as a get-out-of-jail card. But innovation cannot vanquish scarcity and bypass fundamental laws of science. Techno-optimism's main purpose is to avoid confronting the limits of progress, the threats to the existing state of affairs, and the costs of adjustment. Childish solutionism, with its quick fixes, takeaways, action points and deliverables, cannot evade reality. We are the monkeys in the Asian fable, trying to seize the reflection of the moon in the water.

In Shakespeare's *Julius Caesar*, Cassius tells Brutus: 'The fault … is not in our stars / But in ourselves.' Australia's predicament is not preordained by destiny but rather is the result of indolent choices and inaction. Australians need to fundamentally change their mindset. Business as usual now leads nowhere.

The reform agenda is obvious and well known—new inquiries are unnecessary, intelligent detailed proposals have been gathering dust in archives. The economy needs to be realigned and Australia's relationships with the region revisited. The windfalls from periodic resource upturns should be better used given that they are not infinite. Australians need to embrace structural change and work towards a fairer and more equal society. Civic and political participation has to increase. The country must decide whether it is one polity or several. Australians have to force their leaders to lead, let policymakers work on solutions, and hold them to account. Pragmatism is more important than doctrinal purity. Controlled experimentation is essential to test what works. There are no simple or one-size-fits-all solutions.

Living standards might fall but most Australians are highly privileged by global standards. Less may be more, as our lifestyles are increasingly unsustainable in any case. Acceptance that no decision can benefit everyone is fundamental. Sacrifices for the greater good and the future are unavoidable. Divisions based on petty differences are pointless. Australians are resilient and capable when they wish to be, but nothing can be changed until it is faced. It is that kind of time.

The Australian attitudes of 'She'll be right' and 'Punching above our weight' are unhelpful. Critics cannot be dismissed as the doubting Irishman Hanrahan in John O'Brien's poem wrongly warning of 'roon'. Questioning is not pessimism. Wilful ignorance and deliberate blindness are not optimism. Hope is not a solution. Faith cannot erase the facts. Failure isn't fatal but failing to change is.

Donald Horne's phrase 'the lucky country' is today misused by those blind to its irony and criticism of a nation lacking imagination and mired in philistinism, provincialism and its past. Without urgent action, the continuation of Australia's providential good fortune is not assured.

FURTHER READING

Nick Bryant, *The Rise and Fall of Australia: How a Great Nation Lost Its Way*, Random House Australia, 2015.

Andrew Charlton, 'Dragon's Tail: The Lucky Country after the China Boom', *Quarterly Essay*, issue 54, 2014.

Satyajit Das, *A Banquet of Consequences RELOADED: How We Got into the Mess We're in, and Why We Need to Act Now*, Penguin, 2021.

John Edwards, *Reconstruction: Australia after COVID*, Penguin, 2021.

Ross Garnaut, *Superpower: Australia's Low-Carbon Opportunity*, La Trobe University Press, 2019.

Paul Kelly, *The End of Certainty: Power Politics and Business in Australia*, Allen & Unwin, 1994.

McKinsey Global Institute, *Globalization in Transition: The Future of Trade and Value Chains*, 2019.

George Megalogenis, *The Australian Moment: How We Were Made for These Times*, Penguin, 2012.

George Megalogenis, *Australia's Second Chance: What Our History Tells Us about Our Future*, Penguin, 2015.

Laura Tingle, 'Political Amnesia: How We Forgot How to Govern', *Quarterly Essay*, issue 60, 2015.

Laura Tingle, 'Follow the Leader: Democracy and the Rise of the Strongman', *Quarterly Essay*, issue 71, 2018.

Peter Turchin, 'Modelling Social Pressures toward Political Instability', *Cliodynamics*, vol. 4, no. 2, 2013, pp. 241–80.

ACKNOWLEDGEMENTS

I would like to thank Louise Adler for asking me to write this book, Paul Smitz for editing the work and Monash University for publishing it.

IN THE NATIONAL INTEREST

Other books on the issues that matter: